T0338506

LEARNING FROM GOOD AND BAD DATA

THE KLUWER INTERNATIONAL SERIES IN ENGINEERING AND COMPUTER SCIENCES

KNOWLEDGE REPRESENTATION, LEARNING AND EXPERT SYSTEMS

Consulting Editor

Tom Mitchell
Carnegie Mellon University

Other books in the series:

Universal Subgoaling and Chunking of Goal Hierarchies, J. Laird, P. Rosenbloom, A. Newell. ISBN: 0-89838-213-0.

Machine Learning: A Guide to Current Research, T. Mitchell, J. Carbonell, R. Michalski. ISBN: 0-89838-214-9.

Machine Learning of Inductive Bias, P. Utgoff. ISBN: 0-89838-223-8.

A Connectionist Machine for Genetic Hillclimbing, D. H. Ackley. ISBN: 0-89838-236-x.

LEARNING FROM GOOD AND BAD DATA

by

Philip D. Laird
NASA Ames Research Center

KLUWER ACADEMIC PUBLISHERS
Boston/Dordrecht/Lancaster

Distributors for North America:
Kluwer Academic Publishers
101 Philip Drive
Assinippi Park
Norwell, Massachusetts 02061, USA

Distributors for the UK and Ireland:
Kluwer Academic Publishers
MTP Press Limited
Falcon House, Queen Square
Lancaster LA1 1RN, UNITED KINGDOM

Distributors for all other countries:
Kluwer Academic Publishers Group
Distribution Centre
Post Office Box 322
3300 AH Dordrecht, THE NETHERLANDS

Library of Congress Cataloging-in-Publication Data

Laird, Philip D.
  Learning from good and bad data / Philip D. Laird.
    p. cm. — (The Kluwer international series in engineering and
computer science ; 47. Knowledge representation, learning, and
expert systems)
  Bibliography: p.
  Includes index.
  ISBN 0-89838-263-7
  1. Machine learning.   2. Artificial intelligence.   3. Computers.
4. System identification.   I. Title.   II. Series: Kluwer
international series in engineering and computer science ; SECS 47.
III. Series: Kluwer international series in engineering and computer
science. Knowledge representation, learning, and expert systems.
Q325.L35   1988   87-35103
006.3 '1—dc19   CIP

Printed in the United States of America

Contents

List of Figures

ix

PREFACE

This monograph is a contribution to the study of the *identification problem*: the problem of identifying an item from a known class using positive and negative examples. This problem is considered to be an important component of the process of inductive learning, and as such has been studied extensively. In the overview we shall explain the objectives of this work and its place in the overall fabric of learning research.

Context. Learning occurs in many forms; the only form we are treating here is inductive learning, roughly characterized as the process of forming general concepts from specific examples. Computer Science has found three basic approaches to this problem:

- Select a specific learning task, possibly part of a larger task, and construct a computer program to solve that task.

- Study cognitive models of learning in humans and extrapolate from them general principles to explain learning behavior. Then construct machine programs to test and illustrate these models.

- Formulate a mathematical theory to capture key features of the induction process.

This work belongs to the third category.

The various studies of learning utilize training examples (data) in different ways. The three principal ones are:

- Similarity-based (or empirical) learning, in which a collection of examples is used to select an explanation from a class of possible rules.

- Explanation-based learning, in which each example is analyzed individually within the context of a base of knowledge about the domain, the learning goals, and other non-information-theoretic properties. The result of the analysis is then generalized, thereby enlarging the knowledge base.

- Network models of learning, in which large numbers of similar elementary units are interconnected, usually in a fixed topology. The network parameters can be adjusted as examples are presented, until the network as a whole exhibits the desired behavior.

The work described here pertains only to the first approach.

A significant collection of similarity-based theoretical results exists for inferring classes of recursive functions from examples of their values at sample points of the domain. (See, for example, [14], [19], [44].) I shall not adopt this approach. Instead, I prefer to focus on less expressive, more specific domains whose concrete properties can be utilized in constructing the algorithms.

Scope of the Field. The overall goal of this, and related, research is to devise and study good mathematical models of the inductive-inference process. Although many papers with this purpose have been written, the "right" model (by general consensus) has not emerged. What should a good model accomplish? As a minimum, the model should be descriptive of many of the domains and techniques used in artificial intelligence (AI) experiments and applications. And it should be specific enough to permit us to devise algorithms and to reason about their complexity. That this has not yet been done may be illustrated by the fact that there is no general agreement about the requirements of an inductive inference domain, what exactly is meant by a "training example", or what the most appropriate methods are for presenting information.

Once one has proposed such a model, he or she must then determine what the model has to say about previous research, both experimental and mathematical. Inevitably the model will succeed in capturing certain aspects but not others. We often learn as much from the deficiencies of a model as from its successes, for the fact that a particular phenomenon of induction cannot be implemented within the current model implies that the phenomenon entails new ideas and is probably worthy of independent research.

Justification. Judging from the rapid growth of interest in the field, there is little disagreement that inductive learning is an important problem for computer science. Two of the applications most often envisioned for a successful theory are the automatic construction and refinement of large knowledge bases for expert systems and the recognition and classification of data patterns for robotics control software. Apart from these, there is the significant scientific problem of understanding a fundamental and widespread phenomenon such as learning. Even though we cannot even define precisely what learning is, we have a strong sense that there are profound and unifying principles underlying the diversity of behaviors that apparently exhibit some form of learning. To give an analogy, the study of the physics of gases in the mid-nineteenth century proceeded on the basis of the assumption that the many observed laws of gases could be explained by suitably applying the fundamental laws of mechanics. The outgrowth of this idea was the theory of statistical mechanics, which was both mathematically satisfying and useful for engineering applications and further scientific research.

But why a mathematical theory? Are we yet to the point where we understand the problem of inductive learning well enough to formulate it mathematically? To date, theoretical research in inductive inference has played a rather minor part in the design and implementation of computer programs, and it is unlikely that the results in this report will alter this state of affairs.

Nevertheless we need the theory, for these reasons:

- Theory, whether mathematical or not, serves to distill from the mass of experimental details that core of ideas that apply to a more general range of problem settings. A recent critical review of the research noted that "a significant problem in current research on inductive learning is that each research goup is using a different notation and terminology. This not only makes the exchange of research results difficult, but it also makes it hard for new researchers to enter the field." ([22]). Noteworthy cases

where theory *has* identified general concepts include the Version
Space theory of [46], the Model Inference System of Shapiro ([65]),
and the work on approximation by sampling ([71], [15]).

- An essential aspect of theoretical modeling is *simplification*. In exchange for the detail the theory leaves out, one gains the perspective of which ideas should be given priority, the ability to reason
  more clearly about the problem, and the potential to unify phe-
  nomena that would otherwise appear unrelated. An instance of
  this process at work is the research of Shapiro ([66]) in which the
  inductive inference of logical theories, the identification of functions, and the systematic debugging of programs are all shown to
  be closely related.

- Even when the theory contributes nothing to practice, it may
  strongly affect the way we conceptualize the problem. No pro-
  grammer constructing or coding an algorithm refers explicitly to
  the theory of Turing machines (or any other basic model of effective computation). Yet the concept of a finite control with an
  infinite store dominates the way we think about sequential computation.

Organization.   The results that follow are in two parts. Part One de-
velops a model for the identification problem that captures the strategy
of generalization and specialization of hypotheses based on counterexamples. This approach to the identification problem has been the basis
of much research over the years.

Chapter One introduces our formal model of the identification problem, when rules are to be learned in the limit from an arbitrary but

thorough teacher. The model is general enough to apply directly to a
wide class of commonly studied domains.

Chapter Two defines the relations that are used in generalizing and
specializing. For unity we call both the generalizing and the specializing relations *refinement relations*, since they enjoy the same algebraic
properties. We also present general algorithms for the identification
problem using refinements.

Chapter Three considers the problem of designing refinements that
are less general but more useful. To do so, we consider domains with specific, but common, properties and devise relations that take advantage
of these properties. In addition we show how to construct refinement
relations for refinements themselves, and argue that the search for an
appropriate inductive bias can be understood as a process of refinement.

From this theory, we gain the following:

- A clear definition of what constitutes a domain for an identification problem, what we mean by "examples", and a simple charac-
  terization of the operators that are useful for generalization and
  specialization.

- Abstraction of many of the common aspects of different identification algorithms.

- Recognition of some basic limitations of this approach, particularly the fixed representation language and the lack of meaningful
  complexity measures for comparing algorithms.

In Part Two we adopt a different model of the identification problem, one in which examples are drawn independently from an unknown

distribution. Chapter Four defines the model and two criteria for iden-
tication: stochastic identification in the limit, and *pac*-identification as
defined by Valiant ([71]). An advantage of this model is that we can
measure the complexity of identification over many domains. Another
is that the effects of random noise in the examples can be studied: this
is the subject of Chapter Five. From the analysis we reach a clear
understanding of how the strategy of identification from noisy examples generalizes the corresponding strategy for reliable examples. Thus
along with useful mathematical results, such as bounds for the number
of training examples required, we obtain a general conceptual principle
for the design of noise-tolerant identification algorithms.

About the presentation. In order that the contents of this book be
accessible to more than just those in the fields of machine learning and
theoretical computer science, I have chosen to present the mathematical
results with rather more motivational and expository remarks than is
currently fashionable. My hope is that readers will be able follow the
main lines of the development without reading the mathematical details.

Acknowledgments This research has benefitted immeasurably from
the kind assistance of many people. It is my great pleasure to acknowl-
edge their contributions.

Dana Angluin served as my adviser during my four years at Yale.
Lured by the insight and elegance of her work and by her reputation as a
fine teacher, I came to Yale with the hope of studying with her. Despite
the competing demands of family, students, and research, she always
found time to listen to half-formed ideas, wade through poorly written

drafts, and offer numerous suggestions (technical and otherwise).

Dana has also contributed directly to the content of this monograph. In particular, much of Chapter 5 is based on our joint research ([6]). Section 5.6 is mostly her ideas, but because of its relevance she has allowed me to include my version of it here. Also, I have used her (more elegant) proof of Theorem 5.9 in preference to my own. The observations of Section 3.4.1 are primarily Dana's as well.

Neil Immerman and Tom Mitchell bravely agreed to serve as readers, each providing valuable input from the perspective of his own field of expertise.

Conversations with Ranan Banerji, Josh Benaloh, Sandeep Bhatt, Peter Dunning, David Haussler, Neil Immerman, Lenny Pitt, Takeshi Shinohara, and many others during the course of my research were very helpful. At NASA-Ames Roger Bartlett gave generously of his time to help me run off this manuscript. And finally, my colleagues and teachers at Yale endured presentations of these results and provided an environment of friendship and stimulation.

I am grateful to the folks at Kluwer Academic for the opportunity to make my ideas available to a wider readership.

In large part this research was funded by the National Science Foundation, under grants MCS-8002447 and IRI-8404226. Without broad-based funding of this type, the fundamental research so essential to our collective progress would not be possible.

Part I

IDENTIFICATION IN THE LIMIT FROM INDIFFERENT TEACHERS

Chapter 1

THE IDENTIFICATION PROBLEM

This chapter introduces the identification problem and reviews some of the ways it has been studied in the literature. We offer a formal definition for the identification problem and present a familiar, but fundamental, algorithm for identification in the limit.

1.1 Learning from Indifferent Teachers

Inductive learning can be vaguely defined as the process of extracting from large quantities of data a small, finite representation of that data. Of the many smaller subproblems that may comprise this very general problem, we consider only one: the *identification problem*. An informal definition of this problem is as follows:

3

A well-defined class of objects (the *domain*) is fixed, along with a language for representing the objects. A protocol for presenting training instances (*examples*) of an object in the domain is also specified. Often this takes the form of a *teacher* process in which examples and counterexamples of the object are offered *gratis* to the world, in some order. Various kinds of "oracles" capable of answering questions about the object may also be available. The task is to design a *learner* procedure that identifies any object in the class from any acceptable presentation, and uses the representation language to express the result. One assumes that in time the examples are sufficient to rule out any incorrect object in the domain.

Viewing the problem as a protocol between teaching and learning processes tends to introduce some problematic questions about the respective strategies of these participants. If the teacher and learner both want to arrive at a correct hypothesis as quickly as possible, the teacher can simply "tell" the learner, using the examples as an encoding medium. But then, instead of an identification problem, we have a communication problem. Another possibility – that the teacher might seek to frustrate the learner as long as possible – can be realized if the teacher delays a final decision about what object it is presenting until after seeing the learner's guesses, thereby preventing the learner from ever settling on a single hypothesis.

We shall avoid these and similar problems by limiting the presentation to that of an "indifferent" teacher, who first selects the object to be identified, and then chooses a presentation of that object. This presentation remains fixed and independent of the learner's state during the identification process.

In this monograph we shall realize this indifferent teacher in two ways:

1. by assuming that the teacher selects an arbitrary, but correct and exhausive, presentation of the examples before the learner begins the identification algorithm.
2. by assuming that the teacher independently chooses each example at random from an arbitrary, but fixed, distribution of examples not known to the learner.

Part I adopts the first model, and Part II the second. The criteria for successful identification by the learner will necessarily differ in the two cases: in case (1), the learner must emit a correct hypothesis following all but finitely many examples, whereas in case (2) he is required to converge upon a hypothesis with arbitrarily small error, with high probability.

1.2 A Working Assumption

The working assumption of this (and much other) research is that the fundamental theory, inherent limitations, and algorithmic complexity of the identification problem are aspects of the more general phenomenon of inductive learning. Without a definition of inductive learning, we cannot justify this assumption. But the restrictions of the identification problem – e.g., specifying in advance the domain of expression for both teacher and learner; permitting training examples to come only from

highly constrained sources; and disallowing any prior learning experience from the initial conditions – enable us to focus on a reduced set of
aspects that can be studied both experimentally and mathematically.
And where the model fails, questions may be asked that lead to other
approaches to inductive learning.

As justification for focusing on the identification problem, we suggest that actual learning organisms undergo an initial growth period
during which the representations are developed for solving the inductive learning tasks of the local environment. Once this representation
has stabilized, the induction problem becomes an identification problem.
Since the chosen representation (domain) will vary among individuals,
it is important to discover those properties of the identification problem
that are invariant under change of domain. This is the point at which
the model we shall develop here becomes applicable. Important questions about how a domain is chosen will not be addressed.

1.3   Convergence

Any model of the Identification Problem must define what it means for
the learner to identify the item being presented. One such model is
Identification in the Limit , suggested by Gold [24], with the following
scenario. In general the learner receives an unlimited number of (not
necessarily distinct) examples from the teacher. Upon receiving each
example, the learner exhibits a rule representing his current hypothesis (guess) for the item being presented. The learning algorithm is said
to *identify* the item *in the limit* if, after some finite number of examples, the learner's hypothesis is correct (i.e., it does represent the target

item), and thereafter all the learner's hypotheses remain correct. The algorithm is deemed able to identify the class of items if it can identify in the limit any item in that class.

Two things should be noted. First, the learner does not have to determine when he has identified the item; the only requirement is that he will eventually reach that point. Second, there is some flexibility about whether different, but equivalent, rules for the same item represent different guesses. We might, for example, envision a process that identifies a function by presenting a computer program, and constantly modifies the program, but that after some point, the modifications no longer change the actual function it computes. In all the problems we shall consider, however, the learner will be able to converge to a single rule for the item, so that we may require that the learner's hypothesis remain fixed for all but finitely many guesses.

Identification in the limit is perhaps the weakest meaningful criterion for identification. Despite this, it does capture the notion that the learner will eventually discard any false hypotheses, and that in finite time this progression will ultimately converge to a fixed, correct rule. Additional criteria, such as requiring that the hypothesis satisfy some "quality" requirement (e.g., small size), may also be imposed, in order to make the problem more realistic. Questions may also be asked about how long the learner requires to converge (how many examples are required and how much time or space may be required, etc.) In this part we shall not pursue complexity issues, choosing instead to focus on developing the features of the model. (Refer to [21] for a complexity analysis based on recursive function theory.)

1.4   A General Strategy

The Identification Problem has been studied for many different domains, and a number of excellent surveys of these research results are available (especially [8] and [22]). To motivate the theory, we shall examine the main features of some of this research in the next section. Reviewing work in this field, one begins to notice patterns in the various approaches, despite vast differences in the domains.

- The rules are usually represented in an algebraic language whose syntax is fairly simple to present: logic, formal grammars, automata, Boolean algebra, etc.

- Training examples are either presented in or converted to a form that enables the learner to decide whether an example is consistent with a rule.

- The algorithms choose hypotheses that are consistent with the examples seen so far, and revise them only when a counterexample is found.

- Receipt of a counterexample initiates a search through the space of rules for one that is consistent with the counterexample (and often with the previous examples as well).

- A negative counterexample (that is, one which should not agree with the hypothesis but does) causes the search to proceed in the direction of rules that are more specific (i.e., imply fewer examples).

- A positive counterexample (one which should agree with the hypothesis but does not) causes the search to proceed in the direction of rules that are more general (imply more examples).

Not all algorithms fit this paradigm. For example, the extremely general techniques for identifying classes of partial-recursive functions (see [14] and [19]) usually assume only some arbitrary indexing for the class, and thus do not take advantage of any algebraic structure present in the language. And some algorithms (e.g., [3]) utilize deep properties of the domain to keep the amount of searching as small as possible and the efficiency of the algorithm high.

If, however, we were suddenly handed a domain and asked to construct an identification program for it, or if we were to consider how we might instruct a machine to perform such a task automatically, we would probably adopt the strategy of search, generalization, and specialization, in some form. For, even if this does not often lead to efficient implementations, it is effective for a large class of such problems.

1.5   Examples from Existing Research

From the numerous research papers describing inductive inference algorithms for various domains, I have selected a sample in order to highlight the techniques and problems associated with the generalization/specialization approach. The intention thereby is to motivate the subsequent theory, not to document or classify the research in this area.

Algebraic structure of first-order logic.   Robinson [58] suggested using the *subsumption* relation between first-order sentences for machine-based theorem proving. This relation is as follows: if φ_1 and φ_2 are atomic formulas, then $\varphi_1 \geq \varphi_2$ (φ_1 *subsumes* φ_2) if φ_2 is an instance of

φ_1 – i.e., there is a substitution θ such that $\theta(\varphi_1) = \varphi_2$. In the same paper, Robinson exhibited an algorithm for computing the greatest lower bound (with respect to the subsumption ordering $\geq$) for a finite set of atoms. For example, the greatest common instance of the formulas $p(u, u)$ and $p(f(x), f(y))$ is $p(f(z), f(z))$; the substitution that unifies these is $\{u = f(z), x = z, y = z\}$.

The idea of using subsumption as a way of *specializing* formulas follows rather naturally from these ideas. As for *generalization*, Reynolds [57] and Plotkin [51] independently showed how Robinson's unification algorithm could be inverted to compute the least common generalization of a finite set of atoms. (Plotkin also extended this to apply to sets of clauses.) With the ability to specialize and generalize formulas, the next step would be to make inductive inferences by extracting the least common generalization of the set of examples. Efforts toward this end were made, but they did not lead directly to good identification algorithms, mostly because of the failure to relate this syntactical operation to the underlying semantics (model theory). It was Shapiro who supplied this crucial insight much later (see *Logical Theories*, below).

Grammatical Inference. Automata and grammars are frequently used as representations for formal languages; and in both cases, there is a natural notion of generalization and specialization. But the question of what generalization(s) or specialization(s) are appropriate for particular examples has proven to be difficult. In addition, it seems to be easier to decide how to make a specific hypothesis more general than to decide how to make a general hypothesis more specific.

Examples of formal languages are usually in the form of strings, with a tag indicating whether the string is in or out of the language being identified. Given a finite set of strings, it is easy to construct a simple finite-state automaton that accepts only those strings. At any point in the identification procedure, therefore, there is always a consistent hypothesis consisting of the machine that accepts only the finite set of positive examples. Meaningful inductive inferences, however, usually require that this finite set be generalized.

By merging states of a machine, one obtains new machines which accept larger languages. But the choice of which states to merge must be made in some reasonable way, and this has been the source of numerous heuristic approaches. For example, Biermann and Feldman [12] merge, for some fixed parameter k, all states whose behavior on the examples is indistinguishable for strings of length k or less.

When languages are represented as grammars, it is also easy to construct a base grammar which accepts only the strings in a finite set of (positive) examples. Generalizing this very specific grammar can be achieved by merging non-terminal symbols, much like merging states in a machine. In fact, Pao and Carr [49] employ this approach in constructing an identification procedure for regular grammars. From a finite set of strings in the target language, a finite lattice of grammars is derived from the most specific one by merging non-terminal symbols. In order to determine which of these grammars is the most appropriate, the authors select strings which distinguish pairs of grammars, in the sense that the strings are generated by one grammar but not the other. By querying the teacher about the correctness of the string, one grammar of the pair can be selected. Continuing of this procedure, one can identify the target grammer, assuming it is one of the grammars in the lattice.

It is also easy to construct a most general automaton (one which accepts every string over the alphabet). However, specializing an automaton to eliminate negative examples (i.e., strings known *not* to be in the language) is much less straightforward. Similarly, specializing grammars is more difficult than generalizing them, but a general-to-specific approach was suggested by Knobe and Knobe [38]. As their thesis, they state "... that the principle of working from the most general to the most specific is a principle applicable to any inference problem, and it is definitely the prime reason for the success of [their] entire approach." For context-free grammars, a production such as $A \rightarrow B_1 B_2 \ldots B_n$ can be made less general by replacing all occurrences of a non-terminal symbol B_i by a string (of terminals and non-terminals) derivable from B_i. For example, if B derives $d B e$, then one possible specialization of the production $A \rightarrow B C$ is $A \rightarrow d B e C$.

Unfortunately, there is no single most-general production for any non-terminal symbol. Therefore they begin with a very specific grammar that generates only the first example string w in the language: $S \rightarrow w$, where S is the "start" symbol that generates the lang age. When the current grammar fails to generate some string known to be in the language, a search is made for the most general production of the form $S \rightarrow \ldots$ that generates that string. Specialized forms of this production are also computed, and (like Pao and Carr) queries are used to choose the most general production which does not generate strings not in the target language. Specifically, a sample of strings generated by the proposed new production is generated and tested, by querying the teacher about the correctness of these strings. If all are valid strings, the production is added to the language; otherwise, a more specific form of the production is considered. (See [4] and [5] for analysis of the use of queries of this type to direct the identification process.)

The Knobes' algorithm is able to identify only a limited subset of context-free grammars, and no analysis is attempted of the query process for assessing prospective productions. But theirs is noteworthy for its attempt to go from the general to the specific, by contrast with most other algorithms for inferring formal languages. There seems to be something about grammars and automata that makes generalization easier than specialization. For other representations of the same classes of sets, however (e.g., first-order logic [66] and regular algebras [39], specialization is easier, or at least no harder, than generalization. So the preference for generalization or specialization is evidently not a property of the semantic domain.

Conjunctive-form classification. Much of the experimental research into inductive learning has dealt with the "classification learning" or "concept learning" problem. (See [17] for some early pathbreaking research on this problem.) Briefly, examples are given that illustrate members of the class and members not of the class, and the task is to devise a decision rule for the class. Most often the rule is based on a pre-determined set of attributes, each with a finite set of values. For instance, in learning to recognize a particular make and model of car, we would be likely to use the attributes "color", "body-style", "shape of headlights", etc.

Several representations for the classification rules (hereafter called *concepts*) have been adopted, such as decision trees (e.g., [33]) and predicate calculus (e.g., [29]). A difficulty similar to the previously discussed problems of generalizing examples of strings in formal languages arises here: it is always possible to construct a maximally specific concept which accepts only the positive examples presented. Consequently, bottom-up algorithms seeking to avoid overgeneralizing by choosing the least consistent generalization for the training examples will not make generalizations that include more than the positive examples themselves. To avoid this problem, many systems have restricted the rules to conjunctive forms only, disallowing disjunctions such as "(color=red AND body=4door-sedan) OR ...". The resulting "bias" limits expressiveness but eliminates trivial generalizations by fiat. (See [22] for further discussion of work along these lines.)

Unfortunately, more expressive rules incorporating disjunction are usually necessary. Two practical approaches to incorporating disjunction are (1) to incorporate *internal* disjunctions, restricting the use of the operator (e.g., [45]); and (2) to search for several smaller conjunctive rules, each of which explains a subset of the positive examples and eliminates all the negative examples, and then to take the disjunction of these rules (e.g., [46]).

A related technique, designed for efficiency, is the "divide and conquer" algorithm of Quinlan [53]. In his approach, the concepts are represented as decision trees, with attributes on the internal nodes and classes of examples on the leaves. The resulting decision tree can be directly converted to an algorithm that tests attributes of the object and classifies it as + (in the concept class) or − (not in the concept class). Determining the smallest decision tree to describe a set of examples is evidently too difficult, so Quinlan uses an approximation technique. For the root, he chooses the attribute that maximizes the amount of information imparted about the examples. The values of this attribute partition the examples, one block for each value. If the examples in a block are all positive or all negative, the block is represented by a leaf node. Otherwise, the procedure is applied recursively to each block in the partition. Aside from being one of the more efficient techniques for learning concepts, Quinlan's is noteworthy in this context for *not* being based on generalization or specialization.

Version Spaces. Mitchell [46] described a general framework in which the search for a rule consistent with a set of examples can be accomplished. His algorithm is effective for a finite rule space partially ordered according to generality. Thus there is a finite set of most general rules, and a finite set of least general rules.

Assume that one of the rules in the space is exemplified with positive and negative examples. Initially all hypotheses in the space are candidates. Positive examples eliminate hypotheses that are too specific, while negative examples rule out overly general hypotheses. For any set of examples, therefore, there is a subset of the rule space consisting of those rules still consistent with the examples. The intention is that all rules except the target will eventually be eliminated by counterexamples; at that point, the algorithm halts.

Spaces with many rules will consume lots of storage if every candidate rule is represented explicitly. Instead, Mitchell suggests that only two subsets of the rules be retained: the set G of most general hypotheses and the set S of most specific hypotheses consistent with the examples. For each new positive example, those rules in S that do not include the example are replaced by their least generalizations according to the partial ordering; these new rules are in turn tested against the new example, and if necessary, generalized in a similar way. In addition, any rule in G which does not include the positive example is simply discarded. A dual procedure applies in receipt of a negative examples: rules in H may be specialized, while rules in S may be discarded. If a rule in S has been generalized to the point that it is more general than some rule in G, it may be discarded. And dually for rules in H. The termination condition is, then, that G and S both have the same rule and only that rule.

Mitchell's algorithm has been used in several applications, and is noteworthy for its generality and simplicity. The exhaustive, breadth-first search makes it impractical for large rule spaces; and for infinite spaces, it is not effective without modifications. Also, the task of selecting and applying an ordering for the rules may not be straightforward for every domain. Despite these disadvantages, the approach has formed the basis for much of the subsequent work on refinement-based algorithms for inductive inference.

See also [27], [28], and [73] for additional analysis of the Version Space approach.

Logical Theories. Shapiro ([65] and [66]) added a number of original ideas to Mitchell's approach and devised a system that infers sentences in a first-order logical language from examples of their logical consequences. Because of the expressiveness of logic, this method made possible effective identification in the limit of a number of domains, when represented in the syntax of first-order logic. A Prolog implementation of the system was used to demonstrate its usefulness.

Shapiro restricts the form of his sentences to *clause form*, primarily to take advantage of resolution proof procedures. The target of the inference is not a rule (sentence) but a *model* — specifically, an Herbrand model over the language. Examples of this model are expressed as variable-free atomic formulas, signed as either "+" (belonging to the model) or "−" (not belonging)[1]. For example, the sentence

$$(dog(buster)) \land (\forall x \ dog(x) \rightarrow dog(mother(x)))$$

has as positive examples:

dog(buster)
dog(mother(buster))
dog(mother(mother(buster)))
etc.

Negative examples might include *dog(father(buster))*, *cat(buster)*, etc.

The inference algorithm searches for a sentence that characterizes the model. When the current sentence disagrees with an example, an algorithm is invoked that determines whether some clause of the sentence is too specific, or too general, or whether a new clause is needed to account for additional positive facts about the model. In the case of a clause that is too specific, the clause is removed. A clause that is too general is *refined* by making it more specific. More precisely, a list of more specific clauses is generated from the clause and held in queue as candidates for the rule. As additional clauses are needed, clauses in this

---

[1]See the Appendix to Chapter 3 for a summary of logical terminology.

queue are tested in turn. Shapiro proves that this algorithm eventually identifies the target model.

Since the rule space may be infinite, Mitchell's algorithm cannot be applied directly. Instead, Shapiro begins with the most general sentence in the language, and makes it more specific as examples are encountered. An important change from Mitchell's approach is that a careful distinction is made between the rules (syntax) and their models (semantics). Specialization operations are performed on the rules (actually the clauses of the rules). These operations are not necessarily the least consistent specializations, so the algorithm does not proceed breadth first with respect to the semantic; instead, it is breadth first with respect to the syntax. The syntactical ordering (subsumption) and the semantic ordering (subset) are distinct.

Logic, while expressive, is not the most appropriate representation for every problem. One of the main objectives of the research describe here in Part I is to show how Shapiro's ideas apply to other domains as well. We shall find that the most important properties are really algebraic, not logical. Also, Shapiro's algorithm works its way from general to specific. For some applications, specific to general inference is more suitable (e.g., [35]).

1.6   Basic Definitions

The following definitions capture the Identification Problem in the sense we shall use in the first part of this monograph.

Definition 1.1 An *identification problem* is a 4-tuple $\langle (D, \geq), \mathcal{E}, h, GE? \rangle$, where

- D is an arbitrary set of objects partially ordered by $\geq$.

- $\mathcal{E}$ is a recursively enumerable (r.e.) set of expressions representing objects in D.

- $h: \mathcal{E} \to D$ is a mapping from the set of expressions *onto* the set of objects.

- $GE?$ is an oracle for the partial order $\geq$: $GE?(e_1, e_2)$ returns *yes* if $h(e_1) \geq h(e_2)$, and *no* otherwise.

An *instance* of the identification problem is a pair $\langle d_0, EX \rangle$, where

- $d_0 \in D$ is a target element to be identified.

- EX is an oracle that returns *training examples* of d_0, as defined below.

The goal of an identification problem is to construct a learner that, for any instance, finds an expression e_0 such that $h(e_0) = d_0$, whenever the information given by the oracles is correct and "sufficient" (in a sense soon to be made precise). Note that we are adopting the convention of Mitchell and Shapiro and some others that the possible objects for identification are partially ordered. Like Shapiro, we are making explicit the distinction between the syntax $\mathcal{E}$ (often called the *rule space*) and the semantics D. The oracle EX for examples determines how the indifferent teacher presents information about the target d_0, while the oracle $GE?$ supplies the learner with information about the underlying partial order. By means of these oracles, we manage to sidestep the complexity questions associated with computing this information.

Definition 1.2 Let $\mathcal{E}$ be the set of expressions and d_0 the target of an identification problem. A *(training) example* is a signed expression $\langle s, e \rangle$, with $s \in \{+, -\}$ and $e \in \mathcal{E}$, such that

- when s is $+$, then $d_0 \geq h(e)$.

- when s is $-$, then $d_0 \not\geq h(e)$.

Thus in the most general case, *any* expression in $\mathcal{E}$ can be given a sign and presented as an example. In practice, a more restricted class of examples is often sufficient. Many programs receive examples in a representation different from that of the rules; converting this representation into that of the rule syntax is a "folk hack" that has been suggested frequently and is sometimes referred to as the *single-representation trick*.

Definition 1.3 Let S be a set of training examples for d_0. An expression $e \in \mathcal{E}$ is said to *agree with* S if both $h(e) \geq h(s)$ for every $\langle +, s \rangle \in S$ and $h(e) \not\geq h(s)$ for any $\langle -, s \rangle \in S$.

Definition 1.4 A set S of training examples is said to be a *sufficient presentation* for d_0 if, for every $e \in \mathcal{E}$ that agrees with S it is the case that $h(e) = d_0$.

When only a subset X of the complete set of expressions $\mathcal{E}$ is enough to provide a sufficient set of examples for any target object, the oracle EX may be limited to this subset. Also, the query oracle $GE?$ may be limited to answering questions of the form $GE?(e, x)$, where $e \in \mathcal{E}$ and $x \in X$.

Example 1.5 Formal languages are sets of strings over some (finite) alphabet Σ. The natural partial ordering for domains ($\mathcal{D}$) that are sets is containment ($\subseteq$). Languages can be represented syntactically ($\mathcal{E}$) in many ways, including regular expressions, automata, grammars, and string equations. The most common form for training examples are singleton sets (often written as strings). For instance, the positive examples of the set denoted by the regular expression $(1001)^*$ are the strings λ (empty string), 1001, 10011001, ... Any other string is a negative example. In this case, the same class of expressions (single strings) forms a sufficient set of examples for any target set.

The function h maps the expression (grammar, machine, etc.) to the set it denotes. The oracle $GE?()$, when given an expression and a string, decides the membership of that string in the set denoted by the expression. For some domains (e.g., regular expressions, context-free grammars) this is an easy problem, but for others it can be hard or undecidable. $\triangle$

Example 1.6 The term *concept* is often used to describe sets of objects that can be classified by a Boolean expression on a fixed set of attributes. For example, "red-triangle or large-circle" might describe the set of all objects, whose attributes include "color", "shape", and "size", that are either red and triangular or large and circular. A popular syntax for concepts is the class of Boolean expressions in disjunctive normal form over a fixed set of variables (e.g., $x_2 x_5 \bar{x}_6 + x_1 x_3$). The semantic interpretation of such expressions is the set of all truth assignments to the variables that make the expression true. Decision trees (as used by Quinlan) are another common representation. The set of all truth assignments constitutes a complete set of examples; formally, each is expressible as a single minterm, whose complemented variables are assigned a truth value of false and whose uncomplemented variables are assigned a truth value of **true**. Other classes of examples are also possible: for example, the set of prime implicants of the expression (monomials which imply the concept, and for which deleting any variable means that it no longer implies the concept). $\triangle$

Example 1.7 Let $\mathcal{L}$ be a first-order language[2]. A sentence φ in $\mathcal{L}$ can be thought of as denoting the set of Herbrand models in which it is true. If φ is in Horn form, then this set contains a unique smallest model, namely the intersection of all Herbrand models of φ. Thus we can think of φ as denoting its smallest model.

To illustrate, assume that the only unary function symbol in $\mathcal{L}$ is *top*, and consider the sentence $(\forall x)\,red(top(x))$. The smallest model M in which it is valid contains the atoms $red(top(C))$, $red(top(top(C)))$, ..., for every constant symbol C in the language $\mathcal{L}$. The model $M \cup \{red(C)\}$ also satisfies the sentence, but it is a superset of M. As a sufficient set of examples of M, we may take as positive examples all the atoms in M and as negative examples all (ground) atoms not in M. Thus $red(top(C))$ is a positive example, and $red(C)$ is a negative example.

This is basically the domain used by Shapiro [66] for identifying Prolog programs. In his system $\mathcal{D}$ comprised sets of ground atomic formulas over $\mathcal{L}$, partially ordered by containment. $\mathcal{E}$ was the set of Horn sentences over $\mathcal{L}$. The mapping h carried such a sentence to its unique smallest model. $\triangle$

Our final definition states formally what we mean by an (infinite) identification procedure, and what it means for that procedure to identify the domain in the limit.

---

[2]See the appendix to Chapter 3 for a summary of logical notation and terminology.

Definition 1.8 Let $\langle (\mathcal{D}, \geq), \mathcal{E}, h, GE? \rangle$ be an identification problem. $\mathcal{A}$ is called an *identification procedure* for the problem if, for any instance $\langle d_0, EX \rangle$, $\mathcal{A}$ calls EX infinitely often and, following each call, outputs an expression in $\mathcal{E}$. $\mathcal{A}$ is said to *converge* for an instance of the identification problem if there is a rule $e \in \mathcal{E}$ that $\mathcal{A}$ outputs all but finitely many times. Finally, $\mathcal{A}$ is said to *identify* the domain *in the limit* if, for any instance $\langle d_0, EX \rangle$ of the identification problem, $\mathcal{A}$ converges to a rule e such that $h(e) = d_0$.[3]

1.7 A General Algorithm

The following simple algorithm forms the basis for most of the algorithms in Part I. It was first proposed by Gold [24].

Algorithm 1.9 (Identification by Enumeration)
INPUT:

- An r.e. set $\mathcal{E} = e_1, e_2, \ldots$ of expressions.

- An oracle EX for a sufficient set of examples of the target.

- An oracle $GE?$ for information about the ordering.

OUTPUT:

A sequence $H_1, H_2, \ldots$ of guesses, such that each guess H_i is in $\mathcal{E}$ and consistent with the first i examples.

---

[3]In the terminology of [19], the algorithms of Part I perform EX-identification. Furthermore, they are conservative, consistent, and reliable.

PROCEDURE:

1. Initialize: $i \leftarrow 1$.

2. *examples* $\leftarrow$ *emptyset*.

3. Do forever:

    3.1 Call *EX*() and add the example to the set *examples*.

    3.2 While $GE?(e_i, +x) = no$ for some positive example $+x$,
    or $GE?(e_i, -x) = yes$ for some negative example $-x$,
    $i \leftarrow i + 1$.

4. Output e_i (as the current guess). ◇

Theorem 1.10 Algorithm 1.9 identifies the domain in the limit.

PROOF: We must show that the algorithm converges to some expression e, and that e is correct. Suppose the algorithm fails to converge. Then every rule in the enumeration is eventually eliminated by a counterexample. But there is at least one rule e_0 in the enumeration for which no counterexamples occur; thus e_0 can never be eliminated. Thus convergence is certain.

Suppose, then, that the algorithm converges to a rule e. Since, by assumption, the oracle *EX* provides a sufficient set of examples, and since the set *examples* eventually includes any such example, e agrees with every example presented by the oracle. Then by Definition 1.4, $h(e) = d_0$. □

How should we regard Algorithm 1.9? Clearly it is not suitable for implementation as the solution to any practical problem. *Like all algorithms in this monograph, this one is intended to capture an important computational idea, free of the clutter of implementation details.* Here, the main idea is that *any* enumeration of the rule space $\mathcal{E}$ can be used to search for an identifying rule, and that this search will converge correctly. This property is *independent of the domain.* Many running programs are based upon this core idea; but for efficiency, they replace the brute-force search by one that takes advantage of the known properties of the domain.

Yet no matter how the search is implemented, the algorithm will still suffer from three fundamental weaknesses:

- It is not incremental: it must store all its examples.
- It is an infinite process, and the learner has no good way of estimating how close it is to converging.
- It depends strongly upon totally reliable training examples. Any amount of noise – even a single faulty example – can cause the algorithm to fail on some domains.

These inherent weaknesses become clear when the algorithm above is presented, as it is, in its most basic form. They help guide us in deciding what related problems to work on.

Chapters 2 and 3 focus on the search question: how we can accelerate the search by generalization and specialization of rules. The three problems above are addressed in Chapters 4 and 5.

1.8 Additional Comments

We have proposed a simple and yet general model for the identification problem, and a simple (though quite impractical) algorithm for solving it. Note the contrast between identification problems and *search* problems: in the latter, the oracles *EX* and *GE?* are replaced by a single oracle *REL?(e)* which returns information about the relationship between e and d_0. (For example, a binary-search oracle returns *greater*, *less*, or *equal*, according to whether the target object is greater than, less than, or equal to the object presented). Also, in a search problem the routine chooses its own "examples", whereas an identification procedure relies on externally chosen examples. Thus identification and search, while related, are nonetheless distinct problems.

Note also that for every identification problem there is a dual problem in which the partial order $\geq$ is replaced by the inverse relation $\leq$. In this case a positive example would be an expression e such that $d_0 \leq h(e)$.

Finally, it is always possible to change an identification problem on a partially ordered domain $(D, \geq)$ to an equivalent problem in which the domain is a set of sets and the partial order is the containment relation $\supseteq$. To see this, let f be the function which maps $d \in D$ to the set $\{d' \mid d \geq d'\}$. Then it is easy to show that $(D, \geq)$ and $(f(D), \supseteq)$ are isomorphic.

Chapter 2

IDENTIFICATION BY REFINEMENT

We have seen that many identification procedures work by choosing a hypothesis and then generalizing or specializing it in response to counterexamples. We shall now formalize this idea. The key concept is that of a *refinement operator* – this term was used by Shapiro, but the concept is ubiquitous.

From an object $d \in D$, we would like to be able to generalize by computing the set $\{d' \mid d' \geq d\}$, and specialize by computing $\{d' \mid d' \leq d\}$. However, we are constrained to work with the syntax $\mathcal{E}$ rather than directly with D. Refinement operators essentially enable us to perform the same generalization/specialization operations on $\mathcal{E}$.

In this chapter, we shall

- define carefully what a refinement operator is;

27

- modify the fundamental Algorithm 1.9 to take advantage of such an operator; and

- explore the relationship between specific-to-general and general-to-specific identification.

In the next chapter, we shall consider in more detail the problem of constructing useful operators for various domains.

2.1   Order Homomorphisms

In relating the syntax $\mathcal{E}$ to the semantics $\mathcal{D}$, we have imposed only the condition that the mapping h between them be onto $\mathcal{D}$. This condition is clearly required if $\mathcal{E}$ is to be able to express any possible target object. In practice, the syntax is also chosen to reflect some of the structure of $\mathcal{D}$, particularly the ordering $\geq$ on that set. Consequently there is often an ordering $\succeq$ on $\mathcal{E}$ that closely parallels that on $\mathcal{D}$. This ordering [1] need not be a partial ordering, since different expressions e_1 and e_2 may satisfy both $e_1 \succeq e_2$ and $e_2 \succeq e_1$ without being identical. But it can still be used to advantage.

The intuition is that the ordering $\succeq$ on the rule space $\mathcal{E}$ determines when one rule is syntactically more general than ($\succeq$) another. For example, replacing a constant by a variable is a syntactic operation that yields a new rule at least as general as the old. The ordering $\geq$ on the semantics $\mathcal{D}$ determines when one rule *really* represents a more general $\geq$ object than another.

---

[1] An *ordering* is a reflexive and transitive binary relation. It is a *partial* ordering if it is also anti-symmetric. When we wish to emphasise that an ordering is not a partial ordering, we call it a *quasi*-ordering.

The two orderings will usually not be the same. But we shall require that they have the following relationship.

Definition 2.1 . Let $\succeq$ be a recursively enumerable (r.e.) ordering on the set $\mathcal{E}$, and $\geq$ a partial ordering on the set $\mathcal{D}$. The function $h\colon \mathcal{E} \to \mathcal{D}$ is called an *order homomorphism* if $e_1 \succeq e_2$ implies $h(e_1) \geq h(e_2)$ for all e_1 and e_2 in $\mathcal{E}$.

The notion of "equivalent expressions" for the same object d arises from the following equivalence relation:

Definition 2.2 Two expressions e_1 and e_2 in $\mathcal{E}$ are said to be *h-equivalent* if $h(e_1) = h(e_2)$. This equivalence relation will be denoted by $\approx$.

Example 2.3 Let Σ be a fixed alphabet. The class of *pattern languages* over Σ (defined in [2]) is as follows: Let $V = \{x_1, x_2, ...\}$ be disjoint from Σ; the symbols in V are called *variables*. A pattern is an element of $(V \cup \Sigma)^+$. With a pattern p we associate the language $L(p)$ consisting of all strings in Σ^+ obtainable from p by substituting a non-empty string for each variable in p. For example, the pattern $1x1$ over the alphabet $\{0, 1\}$ denotes the language consisting of $101, 111, 1001, 1011, \ldots$ — i.e., all strings of length three or more beginning and ending with 1.

Let $\mathcal{D}$ be the set of pattern languages (over Σ) and $\mathcal{E}$ the set of patterns. The mapping h sends a pattern p to its corresponding language $L(p)$. The natural partial ordering for $\mathcal{D}$ is set containment. An ordering $\succeq$ on $\mathcal{E}$ can also be defined: $p_1 \succeq p_2$ if there exists a substitution $\theta\colon V \to (\Sigma \cup V)^+$ such that $\theta(p_1) = p_2$. For example, $1x1 \succeq 1x_1x_21 \succeq 1x_1x_11 \succeq 1001$. By contrast, $1x_1x_11 \not\succeq 10x_11$, since any substitution changes all occurences of the variable x_1. The ordering $\succeq$ is only a quasi-ordering; for example, $1x_2x_21$ and $1x_1x_11$ are distinct, and yet each is related by $\succeq$ to the other.

It is easy to see that h is an order homomorphism: suppose $w \in L(p_2)$ and $p_1 \succeq p_2$. Then there are substitutions θ and τ such that $\theta(p_1) = p_2$ and $\tau(p_2) = w$. Thus $\tau\theta(p_1) = \tau(\theta(p_1)) = w$, so $w \in L(p_1)$. Hence $L(p_1) \supseteq L(p_2)$. $\triangle$

The syntactic ordering $\succeq$ is a very useful concept that can be used even with rules we don't ordinarily think of as representing a set, as in the following example.

Example 2.4 Let D be the set of rational numbers, and $\mathcal{E}$ the set of ratios p/q, where p and q are integer numerals and $q \neq 0$. Let $h: \mathcal{E} \to D$ map a ratio to the corresponding rational. The ordering $\geq$ with its usual meaning totally orders D. Consider the following ordering for $\mathcal{E}$:

$$\frac{p_1}{q_1} \succeq \frac{p_2}{q_2} \text{ if } p_1 \cdot q_2 \geq p_2 \cdot q_1.$$

This definition assumes that algorithms are available for multiplying and comparing the values of numerals. It is quite evident that h is an order homomorphism. $\triangle$

That h is not in general a bijection accounts for many of the book-keeping difficulties in constructing and using refinement operators. An entirely different set of difficulties arises when the ordering $\succeq$ only partially reflects the ordering $\geq$ on D. For example, when $\succeq$ is the identity relation, h is vacuously an order homomorphism, even though this ordering is trivial and useless for describing most partially ordered sets D.

We cannot expect h to be an isomorphism because of its many-one nature, but the next best property is that h be an *order quasi-isomorphism* (OQI), as follows.

Definition 2.5 Let $\langle \mathcal{E}, \succeq \rangle$ be a quasi-ordered set and $\langle \mathcal{D}, \geq \rangle$ be a partially ordered set. We say that $h \colon \mathcal{E} \to \mathcal{D}$ is an *order quasi-isomorphism* if h is an order homomorphism, and if whenever $h(e_1) \geq h(e_2)$, then $e_1 \succeq e_2$.

Example 2.6 Let X be a fixed set of n Boolean variables (attributes). The set $\mathcal{E}$ of Boolean expressions over X, with connectives $\vee$, $\wedge$, $\to$, and $\sim$ is frequently used as a representation for the set $\mathcal{D}$ of sets of truth assignments to X. Endow $\mathcal{D}$ with the containment ordering, and order $\mathcal{E}$ by logical implication: $e_1 \succeq e_2$ if $\vdash e_2 \to e_1$ (some sound and complete proof system $\vdash$ is assumed). The semantics of the $\to$ connective ensures that h is an order homomorphism. The completeness of $\vdash$ ensures that h is an OQI, since if e_i represents d_i ($i = 1, 2$) and $d_1 \supseteq d_2$, then any assignment satisfying e_2 also satisfies e_1 — i.e., $\models e_2 \to e_1$. Thus $\vdash e_2 \to e_1$. The fact that h is an OQI is one reason why logical representations are so useful. (Other reasons include the regularity of the syntax, and the duality and normal-form properties.)

$$\triangle$$

Example 2.7 The class of *extended* pattern languages [67] is defined similarly to that of pattern languages in Example 2.3, except that substitutions for the variables may include the empty string. Again, the ordering we use on patterns is $p_1 \succeq p_2$ if there is a substitution θ such that $\theta(p_1) = p_2$. $L(p)$ is the language obtained by substituting strings in Σ^*

for variables in p. The mapping from patterns p to languages $L(p)$ is *not* an OQI. For example, when $\Sigma = \{0, 1\}$, $L(x_1 0 1 x_2 0 x_3) \supseteq L(x_1 0 x_2 1 0 x_3)$ (in fact, the languages are equal), but $x_1 0 1 x_2 0 x_3 \not\succeq x_1 0 x_2 1 0 x_3$ and $x_1 0 x_2 1 0 x_3 \not\succeq x_1 0 1 x_2 0 x_3$. However, Shinohara proves ([67], Lemma 2.16) that if $|\Sigma| \geq 3$ and the class $\mathcal{E}$ of patterns is restricted to those in which each variable occurs at most once, then $L(p_1) \supseteq L(p_2)$ iff $p_1 \geq p_2$ — i.e., h is an OQI. $\triangle$

Another way to view an OQI is to collapse the rule set $\mathcal{E}$ into equivalence classes $\mathcal{E}/\approx$. The class $[e] \in \mathcal{E}/\approx$ is the set of all rules e' such that $h(e) = h(e')$. A well-known algebraic theorem [20] states that the mapping $[e]$ to $h(e)$ is bijective. When h is an OQI, we can order the classes as follows: $[e_1] \succeq [e_2]$ iff $h(e_1) \geq h(e_2)$. If h is not an OQI, this ordering may not be well defined. The OQI condition says that the bijection is in fact an isomorphism between $\mathcal{E}/\approx$ and $\mathcal{D}$, preserving the orderings.

Domains for which h is an OQI are very special in that the syntax $\mathcal{E}$ and the semantics $\mathcal{D}$ – while not isomorphic – nevertheless enjoy a very close relationship. This relationship implies, among other things, that refinement operators for these domains have an important duality property that does not hold in general (we shall demonstrate this in the next section). In the next chapter, this "OQI Lemma" will be used in the derivation of a universal refinement.

Henceforth, when $\succeq$ is understood from context, we shall assume that h is an order-homomorphism, unless declared otherwise. (We shall *not* assume that h is an OQI, since many domains of interest do not have this special property.)

2.2 Refinements

2.2.1 Introduction

The term "refinement" has been used to describe a relation which associates with each rule a set of more specific rules. Shapiro [66] was probably the first to consider a variety of refinements for a specific domain (first-order logic). He gave the following definition: A refinement ρ is a mapping from rules to sets of rules such that:

1. For any rule e, $\rho(e)$ is a finite set.

2. If $e_2 \in \rho(e_1)$, then e_1 is "at least as general as" e_2.

3. For any rule e there are no infinite chains $e_1, e_2, \ldots, e_n, \ldots$ such that $e_1 \approx e$ and $e_i \in \rho(e_{i+1})$ for all $i \geq 1$.

He defined refinements for first-order clauses, and included the requisite details about what "more general" and "$\approx$" mean in that domain – details which we do not care to include here.

The elegance of Shapiro's formulation has been widely lauded. For my part, the question about "what is really going on here" seemed paramount, along with the notion that many of the ideas seem not to be inextricably linked to logic, but may apply to other domains equally well.

Shapiro's inference system took advantage of the conjunctive normal form of the sentences; it generalized (i.e., increased the quantity of implied atoms) by conjoining more clauses, and specialized by making the clauses more specific. The refinement operation pertained only to the clauses, and refined in only one direction (general to specific).

These observations raise several more questions: How important is the conjunctive-normal-form property to this identification technique. Can specific-to-general refinements also be used? The whole issue of the relationship between *upward* (specific-to-general) and *downward* (general-to-specific) identification seems important, since certain domains seem to prefer one direction over the other. What properties of the domain affect this apparent preference?

In the remainder of this chapter we shall begin to study these issues; in the next chapter, the specific properties of refinements over certain domains will be reviewed. The ideas I hope will emerge are that refinement operators can be defined and utilized for any well-defined domain; that identification algorithms utilizing these relations extend the simple identification-by-enumeration procedure by separating the searching from the bookkeeping; and that the implementation of refinements entails the design of non-deterministic computational procedures, similar to those used to design algorithms.

2.2.2 Upward and Downward Refinements

Assume that a domain for identification problems has been specified (including a partial ordering $\geq$ on $\mathcal{D}$). The construction of operators for generalizing and specializing the rules in $\mathcal{E}$ begins with choosing an ordering $\succeq$ for $\mathcal{E}$ that is preserved by h. But this alone is not enough: the empty relation and the identity relations are both trivial examples of such an ordering, but neither captures enough of $\geq$ to be useful. Consequently we shall also require a "completeness" property that determines whether $\succeq$ is expressive enough to reflect $\geq$ in the syntax $\mathcal{E}$.

In order to work with this ordering $\succeq$, we shall require that it be recursively enumerable. A *transitive reduction* of $\succeq$ would also be useful: i.e., a minimal sub-ordering $\gamma \subseteq \succeq$ such that the reflexive, transitive closure γ^* is $\succeq$. Then, in order to generalize a rule e we simply enumerate the set $\{e' \mid (e', e) \in \gamma\}$, test these rules, and if necessary, generalize them further using γ. Assuming $\succeq$ is complete, we shall eventually obtain every rule more general ($\succeq$) than e. Similarly, to specialize a rule, we use the inverse relation $\rho = \gamma^{-1}$.

But determining a *minimal* sub-ordering of $\succeq$ can be difficult, and turns out to be unnecessary. In practice it is enough to construct any sub-ordering γ whose reflexive transitive closure γ^* is $\succeq$. A relation such as γ, or its inverse ρ, is what we shall call a *refinement relation*. That these indeed correspond to the generalization/specialization operators in the literature will emerge from the examples.

To summarize, constructing refinement relations for a domain entails finding a suitable ordering $\succeq$ on $\mathcal{E}$ for which h is an order homomorphism between $\mathcal{E}$ and $\mathcal{D}$, and constructing sub-orderings γ and ρ whose closures are $\succeq$ and $\succeq^{-1}$, resp. The formal definitions are given below.

Throughout this section, we shall assume that $\succeq$ is a recursively enumerable ordering on $\mathcal{E}$ such that $h : \mathcal{E} \to \mathcal{D}$ is an order-homomorphism.

Definition 2.8 For any $e \in \mathcal{E}$, let $\mathcal{G}(e)$ be the set $\{e' \mid e' \succeq e\}$. The ordering $\succeq$ is said to be *semantically complete for e* if $h(\mathcal{G}(e)) = \{d \mid d \geq h(e)\}$. If $\succeq$ is semantically complete for all $e \in \mathcal{E}$, then $\succeq$ is called a *semantically complete* ordering.

Intuitively, completeness of $\succeq$ means that by enumerating the set of all rules above e in the ordering $\succeq$, we obtain at least one rule for every semantic element in D above $h(e)$.

Definition 2.9 An *upward refinement* γ is a recursively enumerable binary relation on $\mathcal{E}$ whose reflexive, transitive closure γ^* is the relation $\succeq$. If $\succeq$ is semantically complete (for e), then γ is likewise said to be semantically complete (for e).

Many heuristic operators in the literature serve as generalization operators, but the issue of their completeness for the rule space is seldom considered. With the two preceding definitions, we can now characterize precisely what this means.

Note that the ordering $\succeq$ and the refinement γ are closely tied. Often it is easier to characterize the syntactic ordering locally (with γ) than globally; in this case we construct γ first, and simply define $\succeq$ to be the closure. In this case, a necessary condition on γ is that if $(e_1, e_2) \in \gamma$ then $h(e_1) \geq h(e_2)$.

The notation $\gamma(e)$ will be used to denote the set $\{e' \mid (e', e) \in \gamma\}$. When viewing γ as a function in this way, we shall refer to γ as a *refinement operator*.

Note that we, unlike Shapiro, make no assumptions about the finiteness of $\gamma(e)$ or about the length of chains in the ordering $\succeq$.

Example 2.10 Let D be the class of regular subsets of some finite alphabet $\Sigma = \{\sigma_1, \ldots, \sigma_n\}$, and $\mathcal{E}$ the regular expressions over Σ. $\mathcal{E}$ is an algebra whose expressions are constructed from the constants $\sigma_i \in \Sigma$ and ϕ, the binary operations $+$ (union) and $\cdot$ (concatenation), and the unary operation * (Kleene closure). The association between a regular expression and its corresponding regular set is well known [31].

Let R, R_1, R_2, ... be variables for regular expressions over the alphabet $\Sigma = \{\sigma_1, \ldots, \sigma_n\}$. $R_1 \xrightarrow{\gamma} R_2$ means that $(R_2, R_1) \in \gamma$. All rules are implicitly quantified universally over the variables.

$R \xrightarrow{\gamma} (R + R)$.

$\phi \xrightarrow{\gamma} (\phi \cdot \phi)$.

$R \xrightarrow{\gamma} (R)^*$.

$\phi \xrightarrow{\gamma} \sigma_i$, for $1 \leq i \leq n$.

If $R_1 \xrightarrow{\gamma} R$, then $(R_1 + R_2) \xrightarrow{\gamma} (R + R_2)$.

If $R_1 \xrightarrow{\gamma} R$, then $(R_1 + R_2) \xrightarrow{\gamma} (R_2 + R)$.

If $R_1 \xrightarrow{\gamma} R$, then $(R_1)^* \xrightarrow{\gamma} (R)^*$.

If $R_1 \xrightarrow{\gamma} R$, then $(R_1 \cdot R_2) \xrightarrow{\gamma} (R \cdot R_2)$.

If $R_2 \xrightarrow{\gamma} R$, then $(R_1 \cdot R_2) \xrightarrow{\gamma} (R_1 \cdot R)$.

Figure 2.1: Upward refinement for regular expressions.

Red'ko has shown that h-equivalence of regular expressions cannot be defined using equational logic [55]; however, non-equational finite axiom schemes are known [60].

In Figure 2.1 we define an upward refinement for regular expressions. For legibility the notation $\alpha \xrightarrow{\gamma} \beta$ is used to mean that $(\beta, \alpha) \in \gamma$, or equivalently, $\beta \in \gamma(\alpha)$. The syntactic ordering $\succeq$ is γ^* by definition.

For example, $\gamma(\sigma_1)$ consists of two expressions: $(\sigma_1 + \sigma_1)$ (applying the first rule, with $R = \sigma_1$) and $(\sigma_1)^*$ (via the third rule).

It is easy to see that h is an order-homomorphism for the ordering $\succeq$ — i.e., for each relation $\alpha \xrightarrow{\gamma} \beta$, the regular set $h(\beta)$ includes the regular set $h(\alpha)$. Also, it is an easy exercise to show that, starting from the expression ϕ, any regular expression R over Σ can be obtained in a finite number of "refinement steps":

$$\phi \xrightarrow{\gamma} R_1 \xrightarrow{\gamma} \ldots \xrightarrow{\gamma} R.$$

For example, a derivation of $(\sigma_1 + \sigma_2)^*$ is as follows:

$$
\begin{aligned}
\phi \;\; &\xrightarrow{\gamma} \;\; (\phi + \phi) \\
&\xrightarrow{\gamma} \;\; (\sigma_1 + \phi) \\
&\xrightarrow{\gamma} \;\; (\sigma_1 + \sigma_2) \\
&\xrightarrow{\gamma} \;\; (\sigma_1 + \sigma_2)^*.
\end{aligned}
$$

Thus γ is a semantically complete upward refinement for ϕ.

However, γ is *not* complete for all expressions. For example, the regular set $\{\sigma_1, \sigma_2\}$ is more general than (i.e., , contains) the set $\{\sigma_1\}$; however, no regular expression for $\{\sigma_1, \sigma_2\}$ can be derived with γ from the expression $R = \sigma_1$.

A very simple, not to say practical, refinement that *is* semantically complete can be formulated using the *h*-equivalence relation ($\approx$):

$$\text{if } (R_1 + R_2) \approx R_2, \text{ then } R_1 \xrightarrow{\gamma} R_2.$$

Since $\approx$ is r.e., we can enumerate the expressions R_2 such that $R_1 \xrightarrow{\gamma} R_2$, for any expression R_1. Furthermore, if R_1 is a regular expression designating the set S_1, and if R_2 is a regular expression whose corresponding set S_2 includes S_1, then $R_1 + R_2$ represents the set $S_1 \cup S_2 = S_2$, so $R_1 + R_2 \approx R_2$. So the above refinement rule says that R_2 is in $\gamma(R_1)$, and it follows that γ is semantically complete. (In fact, $\succeq = \gamma^* = \gamma$.) $\triangle$

The inverse of $\geq$ on $\mathcal{D}$ is a partial ordering which we denote by $\leq$. Similarly, $\preceq$ denotes the ordering inverse to $\succeq$ on $\mathcal{E}$. We then have the following dual definition.

Let $R, R_1, R_2, \ldots$ be variables for regular expressions over the alphabet $\Sigma = \{\sigma_1, \ldots, \sigma_n\}$. $R_1 \overset{\rho}{\to} R_2$ means that $(R_2, R_1) \in \rho$. Rules are implicitly quantified universally.

$R \overset{\rho}{\to} (R + R)$.

$R^* \overset{\rho}{\to} (R^* \cdot R^*)$.

$R^* \overset{\rho}{\to} (R^*)^*$.

$\sigma_i \overset{\rho}{\to} \phi$, for $1 \leq i \leq n$.

$R^* \overset{\rho}{\to} R$

If $R_1 \overset{\rho}{\to} R$, then $(R_1 + R_2) \overset{\rho}{\to} (R + R_2)$.

If $R_1 \overset{\rho}{\to} R$, then $(R_1 + R_2) \overset{\rho}{\to} (R_2 + R)$.

If $R_1 \overset{\rho}{\to} R$, then $(R_1)^* \overset{\rho}{\to} (R)^*$.

If $R_1 \overset{\rho}{\to} R$, then $(R_1 \cdot R_2) \overset{\rho}{\to} (R \cdot R_2)$.

If $R_2 \overset{\rho}{\to} R$, then $(R_1 \cdot R_2) \overset{\rho}{\to} (R_1 \cdot R)$.

Figure 2.2: Downward refinement for regular expressions.

Definition 2.11 A *downward refinement* ρ is a recursively enumerable (r.e.) binary relation on $\mathcal{E}$ whose reflexive-transitive closure ρ^* is the relation $\preceq$. If $\preceq$ is semantically complete (for e), then ρ is likewise said to be semantically complete (for e).

The notation $\rho(e)$ will be used to denote the set $\{e' \mid (e', e) \in \rho\}$, when we view ρ as an operator.

Example 2.12 In Figure 2.2 we give a downward counterpart to that of Figure 2.1. It is semantically complete for the expression $(\sigma_1 + \ldots + \sigma_n)^*$, but not in general. A complete downward refinement is:

$$\text{if } (R_1 + R_2) \approx R_2, \text{ then } R_2 \overset{\rho}{\to} R_1.$$

$\triangle$

Example 2.13 Based on the total ordering $\succeq$ defined above for the rationals (Example 2.4), we can construct an upward refinement γ in a variety of ways. One simple way, based on the fact the the rationals are enumerable, is to define $\gamma(p/q)$ to be the set of all ratios r/s such that $rq > ps$. A sparser refinement is as follows:

$$\gamma(p/q) = \begin{cases} \{1/1, 1/2, \ldots, 1/n, \ldots\}, & \text{if } p = 0 \\ \{y/x \mid y > 0, x = \lceil \frac{qy}{p} - 1 \rceil \}, & \text{otherwise.} \end{cases}$$

For example, $\gamma(1/3) = \{1/2, 2/5, 3/8, \ldots\}$. To see that γ^* is $\succeq$, suppose p/q is given, $q \neq 0$, and $p'/q' \succ p/q$. For the case $p \neq 0$, a sequence of refinements from p/q to p'/q' can be constructed as follows: $p'/z \in \gamma(p/q)$, where $z = \lceil qp'/p - 1 \rceil$. Note that $z \geq q'$: since $p'q > q'p$, we have $p'q/p > q'p/p = q'$. If $z = q'$, we're done. Otherwise, we continue refining as follows: $p'/z \rightarrow p'/(z-1) \rightarrow \ldots \rightarrow p'/q'$. For the case $p = 0$, first refine $p/q \rightarrow 1/n$, where $p'/q' \succ 1/n$. Then use the preceding construction to refine our way from $1/n$ to p'/q'.

Many other refinements for this domain are possible. In the next chapter, we give one for which $\gamma(p/q)$ is a finite set, for all ratios p/q.

Of course, we are unlikely to want to construct an identification algorithm for rationals. The point of this example is that the concept of a refinement operator is applicable, not just to "classical" domains such as predicate calculus and formal languages, but to any domain with the structural properties of Definition 1.1. $\triangle$

Clearly, the inverse of any upward refinement is a downward refinement for the inverse ordering. However, not every property of an upward refinement holds for its inverse, and conversely. The only property of refinements that we have considered so far is semantic completeness, and

For this domain, γ is complete but γ^{-1} is not. The domain $\mathcal{D}$, with three elements $d_1 > d_2 > d_3$, is represented by $\mathcal{E}$ with five elements: one mapping to d_3 and two each to d_2 and d_1. In the diagram below, h-equivalent elements of $\mathcal{E}$ are shaded; edges depict the relation γ.

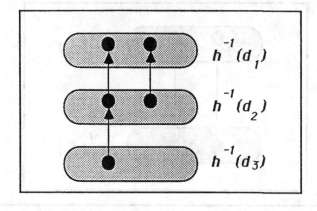

Figure 2.3: A Counterexample.

in Figure 2.3 we illustrate a domain for which γ is complete but γ^{-1} is not: searching downward from the rightmost element in $h^{-1}(d_1)$, we will not encounter any rule representing d_3.

For logical and other domains in which h is an OQI, we have the following:

Lemma 2.14 When h is an OQI from $\langle \mathcal{E}, \succeq \rangle$ to $\langle \mathcal{D}, \geq \rangle$, then every refinement and its inverse are semantically complete.

PROOF: Let e_1 be any formula and d any element $\geq h(e_1)$. To show that an upward refinement γ is semantically complete, we need to show that some $e \in \gamma^*(e_1)$ satisfies $h(e) = d$. But since h is an OQI, $\mathcal{E}/_\approx$

For this domain, γ and γ^{-1} are complete, but h is not an OQI. $\mathcal{D}$, with two elements $d_2 > d_1$, is represented by $\mathcal{E}$ with four elements: two mapping to d_2 and two to d_1. In the diagram below, h-equivalent elements of $\mathcal{E}$ are shaded; edges depict the relation γ.

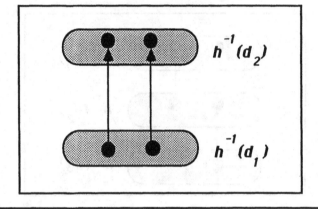

Figure 2.4: Another Counterexample.

is isomorphic to $\mathcal{D}$, there must be an h-equivalence class C such that $C \succeq [e_1]$ and $h(C) = d$. But for any $e \in C$, $e \succeq e_1$.

The argument for a downward refinement is completely dual. Since the inverse of a refinement is also a refinement, the result is proved. $\square$

Figure 2.4 illustrates that the converse does not hold: both a refinement and its inverse can be semantically complete even though there is no OQI between $\mathcal{E}$ and $\mathcal{D}$. To see that the map h is not an OQI, let e_1 be the leftmost rule in $h^{-1}(d_1)$ and e_2 be the rightmost rule in $h^{-1}(d_2)$; although $d_2 \geq d_1$, e_2 cannot be reached by generalization from e_1.

2.2.3 Summary

The principal ideas of this section, stated informally, are as follows:

1. To be useful, an ordering $\succeq$ on the rule space needs to satisfy a completeness property. This property says that if we look at all rules more general than e we will examine enough rules to represent any semantic object more general than the one that e represents.

2. To generalize, we need a computable operator γ. To specialize, we use ρ. The inverse of a generalizing operator is a specializing one, and vice versa.

3. What γ does for us is to enable us to compute $\succeq$ a few rules at a time. Thus if the rule e is known to be too specific, we may eventually want to compute every rule more general than e. By first finding $\gamma(e)$, then applying γ to all of these rules, and so forth, we should eventually obtain all rules $\succeq e$. And we do so by proceeding (in some sense) from specific to general.

4. Special domains, the OQI's, for which the syntax and semantics are closely related, have a very useful property: every refinement is complete. The importance of this idea will emerge later.

By being precise about these concepts, we gain the ability to verify the suitability of our operators and to design domain-independent algorithms using them.

2.3   Identification by Refinement

Refinement relations enable us to modify the basic Algorithm 1.9 to take advantage of the ordering on the domain. With the ordering comes the notion of upward and downward directions, so algorithms for both directions are given. The algorithms are not especially simple. And, somewhat surprisingly, they are not duals. The symmetry between up and down is broken by the examples, since by definition positive examples are always below ($\leq$) the target d_0. This means that the upward (generalizing) algorithm is less complex than the downward, in the general case where we assume nothing more than the existence of semantically complete refinements for the domain.

Both algorithms are rather complex, because of the generality of the setting. As such they are only of theoretical interest. In Chapter 3 we set about to make them more useful.

Upward-Refinement Algorithm.   We assume that there are procedures available for enumerating the rules $\mathcal{E}$ in some arbitrary order and for enumerating $\gamma(e)$ for any $e \in \mathcal{E}$. The algorithm has two phases. At first, it essentially copies Algorithm 1.9, taking the first hypothesis that agrees with all examples seen so far. This phase continues until a positive example $+x$ is received. The expression x represents a lower bound for the target d_0; and since γ is complete, $\gamma^*(x)$ is sure to contain an expression e_0 for the target.

Note that, like Algorithm 1.9, the algorithm is *conservative* (rejects a hypothesis only when shown a counterexample) and *consistent* (always outputs a hypothesis correct for the portion of the presentation it has received). If no positive example is received, the algorithm *is* the latter algorithm. (Therefore it would be best if the enumeration of $\mathcal{E}$ began with rules for which there are no positive examples.)

Algorithm 2.15 (Identification by Upward Refinement)

Notation: $\gamma(e \mid n)$ denotes the expression, if any, output on the n'th step of the enumeration of $\gamma(e)$. $\gamma(e \mid 0) = e$ for all e; and while $\gamma(e \mid n)$ may not yield any expression for a particular value of n, we are sure that every expression in $\gamma(e)$ is $\gamma(e \mid n)$ for some n.

INPUT:

- An enumeration $\mathcal{E} = e_1, e_2, \ldots$ of the rules.

- A semantically complete upward refinement, γ.

- An oracle $GE?$ for information about the ordering.

- An oracle EX for a sufficient set of examples of the target.

OUTPUT:

A sequence $H_1, H_2, \ldots$ of guesses, such that each guess H_i is in $\mathcal{E}$ and is consistent with the first i examples.

PROCEDURE:

1. $Q \leftarrow emptyqueue$. (Queue elements are pairs, $[e, n]$, where $e \in \mathcal{E}$ and $n \geq 0$.)

2. $examples \leftarrow emptyset$. (Save all examples.)

3. $i \leftarrow 1$. (Count examples.)

4. $H \leftarrow e_1$. (Initialize current hypothesis H to first expression in the enumeration.)

5. Repeat

    5.1 Call $EX()$ for a new example, x.

    5.2 Add x to *examples*.

    5.3 If x is a negative example, then

        5.31 Comment: (So far we have gotten only negative examples.)

        5.32 while *too_general*(H),

           5.321 $i \leftarrow i + 1$

           5.322 $H \leftarrow e_i$

        5.33 Output H

until x is a positive example.

6. Comment: (At last we have a lower bound x for the target and we can start refining our way upward.)

7. Add $[x, 0]$ to Q. (x is a possible hypothesis.)

8. Do forever

    8.1 While H disagrees with some example

        8.11 If *too_specific*(H) and not *too_general*(H), then add $[H, 1]$ to Q. (Schedule H for refinement.)

        8.12 $H \leftarrow next\_hypothesis()$.

    8.2 Output H

    8.3 Add an example $EX()$ to *examples*

Here, *next_hypothesis*() is:

Repeat

    1. Remove the next entry from the head of Q. Let it be $[e, n]$
       (representing $\gamma(e, n)$).

    2. If $n > 0$, then add $[e, n + 1]$ to Q. (To continue dovetailing
       the refinement.)

    3. $H \leftarrow \gamma(e \mid n)$ (This may or may not yield an expression.)

until H has a new value.

And *too_specific*(H) is:

If $GE?(H, e) = no$ for some positive example $+x \in examples$,

then return **true** else return **false**.

And *too_general*(H) is:

If $GE?(H, e) = yes$ for some negative example $-x \in examples$,

then return **true** else return **false**.   ◇

Theorem 2.16 Algorithm 2.15 identifies the domain in the limit.

PROOF: The algorithm tests its current hypothesis H against every example. With our assumptions about the sufficiency of the examples, we can conclude that if H is incorrect, it will eventually be discarded. We need only show that the algorithm eventually makes a correct rule its current hypothesis.

Suppose the target object d_0 is minimal with respect to $\geq$, so that there may be no positive examples. Then the algorithm will never escape from the **repeat** loop. But this loop coincides with that of Algorithm 1.9, which we already have shown to converge correctly.

Otherwise, a positive example $+x$ does occur. It will become the hypothesis H if the hypothesis current at the time x is received is ever discarded. All subsequent hypotheses are γ-refinements of this expression, which we shall label r_0. Completeness of γ ensures that there is a smallest integer $n \geq 0$, and a chain of rules $r_0, \ldots, r_n$ such that $h(r_n) = d_0$, and for all $0 \leq i < n$, $r_i \in \gamma(r_{i-1})$. The computation of $\gamma(r)$ for the various expressions r in $\gamma^*(r_0)$ is dovetailed with the enumeration of examples. We know, however, that there are integers $k_1, \ldots, k_n$ (assumed to be as small as possible) such that $r_{i+1} = \gamma(r_i \mid k_{i+1})$ for $0 \leq i < n$. k_{i+1} represents the number of computation steps required to compute r_{i+1} from r_i using γ.

Assume the algorithm never converges. Then every hypothesis is eventually discarded. We argue that r_n must eventually become the current hypothesis. This leads to the contradiction that r_n, a correct hypothesis, must be discarded. It will then follow that the algorithm converges, and the proof will be complete.

We argue by induction that r_i eventually becomes the hypothesis H, for $0 \leq i \leq n$. For r_0 this is true by assumption. Assume r_i is the hypothesis $(i < n)$. Since $h(r_n) > h(r_i)$, the only counterexample for which r_i will fail is a positive example (for which r_i will be too specific). Thus $[r_i, 1]$ is added to Q. Q remains finite; and since, by assumption, every hypothesis is ultimately discarded, the routine *next_hypothesis* is called infinitely often. Hence $[r_i, 1]$ will reach the front of the queue, and $[r_i, 2]$ will be placed on the end. Continuing the argument in this fashion, we conclude that $[r_i, j]$ will be enqueued for all $j \geq 1$ and will make its way to the front of the queue, to be considered as the next hypothesis. In particular, $[r_i, k_{i+1}]$ will reach the front, and the next hypothesis will be $\gamma(r_i, k_{i+1})$, which is just r_{i+1}.

We conclude that r_n will eventually become H. $\qquad\qquad\qquad\Box$

Downward Refinement Algorithm Unlike the upward direction, the downward algorithm never receives any expression in the examples that it knows is an upper bound for the target. The positive examples are known to be below the target, while the negative examples may include expressions incomparable to the target. Thus the most it can do is refine downward every expression not known to cover a negative example. Since there may be no negative examples, it must also dovetail an enumeration of $\mathcal{E}$. Of course, it would converge with only this enumeration (it is then pure identification by enumeration), but presumably the refinement increases the likelihood that it will converge more rapidly. In all, however, the downward refinement algorithm is considerably more involved and decidedly less satisfactory than the upward algorithm.

Algorithm 2.17 (Identification by Downward Refinement)

Notation: $\rho(e \mid n)$ denotes the expression, if any, yielded in exactly n computation steps of the enumeration of $\rho(e)$. $\rho(e \mid 0) = e$.

INPUT:

- An enumeration $\mathcal{E} = e_1, e_2, \ldots$ of the rules.

- A semantically complete downward refinement, ρ.

- An oracle $GE?$ for information about the ordering.

- An oracle EX for a sufficient set of examples of the target.

OUTPUT:

A sequence $H_1, H_2, \ldots$ of guesses, such that each guess H_i is in $\mathcal{E}$ and is consistent with the first i examples.

PROCEDURE:

1. $Q \leftarrow emptyqueue$. (Queue elements are pairs, $[e, n]$, where $e \in \mathcal{E}$ and $n \geq 0$.)

2. $examples \leftarrow emptyset$. (Save all examples.)

3. $i \leftarrow 1$. (Count examples.)

4. $H \leftarrow e_1$. (Initialize current hypothesis H to first expression in the enumeration.)

5. Do forever

    5.1 Add an example $EX()$ to $examples$.

    5.2 While H disagrees with some example,

        5.21 $i \leftarrow i + 1$

        5.22 Add $[e_i, 0]$ to Q. (Dovetail the enumeration of $\mathcal{E}$ with the refining.)

        5.23 If $too\_general(H)$ and not $too\_specific(H)$, then add $[H, 1]$ to Q (Begin refining H.)

        5.24 $H \leftarrow next\_hypothesis()$

    5.3 Output H

Here, $next\_hypothesis$ is:

Repeat

    1. Remove the next entry from the head of Q. Let it be $[e, n]$.

    2. If $n > 0$ then add $[e, n + 1]$ to Q. (Continue dovetailing.)

    3. $H \leftarrow \rho(e \mid n)$. (This may or may not yield an expression.)

until H has a new value.

    Procedures *too_general* and *too_specific* are the same as in Algorithm 2.15.   ◇

Proposition 2.18 Algorithm 2.17 identifies the domain in the limit.

    Since Algorithm 1.9 is embedded in the algorithm, this theorem is immediate. The refinement activity is purely an enhancement.

Observations. The two algorithms above share some common aspects with Mitchell's candidate-elimination algorithm (see *Version Spaces* in Section 1.5), and yet the refinement approach is quite different, for the following reasons.

- In the most basic Version-Space model, no distinction is made between semantics and syntax. In effect, the two are assumed to be isomorphic. As a result, generalization (and specialization) in the rule space are taken to be the least consistent generalization (resp., specialization). In a domain whose syntax is more complex, this type of "least inconsistent" refinement is usually inefficient, and often impractical. And for an infinite domain, we encounter the infamous "disjunction problem", wherein each least inconsistent

generalization adds a finite number of examples to the scope of
a rule, without ever converging to a target rule that covers an
infinite number of examples.

Refinement operators do not try to make the least generalization.
Instead they use the order properties of the syntax in order to
make whatever generalizations they can from the form of the rule.
For example, the regular expression refinement given earlier generalizes the string a to a^* — clearly not a least generalization.

- In order to converge, the Version-Space model assumes that the
  domain is a finite partial-ordering. The refinement model handles
  infinite domains, and admits quasi-orderings.

- Mitchell's algorithm retains all the G (most general, consistent
  rules) and S (most specific, consistent rules) explicitly in storage.
  The refinement algorithms above retain rules that are too specific
  and not too general (or $v.v.$ in the downward case), for subsequent
  generalization (refinement). In both cases, the storage requirements for potential hypotheses and retained examples grow very
  rapidly.

- The candidate-elimination algorithm halts when only a single candidate remains. The refinement algorithms, by contrast, are infinite procedures which do not "know" when they have converged,
  only that they eventually will do so.

Note also that we are intentionally ignoring an issue that arises
whenever a learning system is designed: of all consistent generalizations of the examples, which is the most appropriate? Often ancillary
considerations come into play here – the simplicity of the rule, its logical justification, and so on. We have the luxury of treating only the

theoretical aspects of the problem and avoiding the more philosophical ones.

2.4   Conclusion

The preceding algorithms are certainly too clumsy to be of practical importance. Their significance arises from the need to determine the minimal requirements for refinement operators. Comparing other definitions, such as Shapiro's (Section 2.2.1), with Definition 2.9, we see how much more general (and yet simple) our definition is. Such generality is justified only if there are algorithms that can utilize it. The algorithms of the preceding section provide some justification.

The next task is to shed generality in favor of practicality, and consider how to construct, verify, and utilize refinement operators.

Chapter 3

How to Work With Refinements

3.1 Introduction

Having presented the fundamental concepts and some elementary algorithms for identification using refinements, we now need to know how to use refinements in more sophisticated ways. The paradigmatic situation is that we are faced with constructing an identification program on an unfamiliar domain. Armed with the ideas of the previous chapter, we should

1. select a representation $\mathcal{E}$ for the class of target objects $\mathcal{D}$, and the mapping h that relates them.

2. prepare an ordering $\succeq$ on $\mathcal{E}$ that relates to the ordering $\geq$ on $\mathcal{D}$ as closely as possible and which is preserved by h.

55

3. construct a refinement ρ and/or γ for the ordering.

4. plug these into a nifty, all-purpose algorithm for identification.

The algorithms in Chapter II are effective but only of theoretical interest. One would benefit from a library of algorithms that can take advantage of the properties of the particular domain and its refinements. We shall see that it is usually easy to construct and verify an algorithm; constructing and verifying a refinement is more difficult. One of the goals of this chapter is to suggest techniques for designing refinements.

A theme to bear in mind is that constructing refinements is very much like writing programs. In this case, the programming language being used is the algebraic language of $\mathcal{E}$; the operational semantics of the language is the proof system (equational logic, term-rewriting system, etc.) used to verify properties of algebraic formulas on $\mathcal{E}$; and the model-theoretic semantics is the mapping h from $\mathcal{E}$ to $\mathcal{D}$. The main result of this chapter is the establishment of a "universal refinement" that plays a role similar to that of the universal function in recursive models of computation [42].

Despite our chat about "more practical" issues, to the researcher concerned with designing machine systems that learn, the results of this chapter will still be quite theoretical. The most useful idea is that refinement operators (the routines that generalize and specialize rules) are not mysterious: they have simple algebraic properties and help manipulate rules in predictable ways. They also separate out the search aspects of inductive learning, and help to identify those parts of the problem that are domain-independent.

Throughout this chapter the ideas will be developed for upward refinements (γ) only, whenever they apply equally well to both upward and downward refinements. Where the two directions differ in some significant way, the differences will be noted.

3.2 Three Useful Properties

Most of the complexity in Algorithms 2.15 and 2.17 comes from the need to dovetail the computation of $\gamma(e)$ or $\rho(e)$ with the enumeration of the presentation EX. Also, a lot of unnecessary work is done when the refinement, applied to e, generates a large number of expressions h-equivalent to e and then performs redundant tests of them as possible hypotheses after having previously rejected e. And clearly the least satisfactory aspect of the algorithms is that they rely on Algorithm 1.9 as backup in case no valid expression e_0 is $\gamma^*(e)$ or $\rho^*(e)$ for any e.

In practice, all of these can be avoided for most domains, and the algorithms can be drastically simplified as a result. The price to be paid is that the refinements may be more difficult to construct and prove. In this section, we define three special properties and show how they either simplify or accelerate induction by refinement.

Definition 3.1 A refinement γ is said to be *locally finite* if, for all $e \in \mathcal{E}$, the set $\gamma(e) = \{e' \mid (e', e) \in \gamma\}$ is finite and computable – i.e., there is an algorithm that, for input e, computes $\gamma(e)$ and halts.

Intuitively, a locally finite refinement is one for which there is a procedure that takes any expression e, computes $\gamma(e)$ and halts. When a refinement is locally finite, the identification algorithm does not have to dovetail the computation of $\gamma(e)$ with the rest of the (infinite) identification process.

A trick that often helps to convert a refinement γ into a locally-finite refinement γ' is to define $\gamma'(e)$ to be the set of expressions in $\gamma(e)$ of *size* at most c greater or smaller than the size of e; here, c is a fixed positive integer, and for any e and any integer s the set of expressions of size at most s is finite. Provided a suitable c can be found and there is an algorithm to list all expressions in $\gamma(e)$ less than a given size, we can construct a locally-finite refinement γ' from γ.

Example 3.2 Let $X = \{x_1, \ldots, x_n\}$ be a set of propositional variables, and let $\mathcal{E}$ be the algebra of Boolean expressions on X formed from the constants **true** and **false** and the connectives $\neg$ (not), $\vee$ (or) and $\wedge$ (and). As in Example 2.6, the meaning $h(e)$ of a Boolean formula e is taken to be the set of satisfying truth assignments, partially ordered by containment. $\mathcal{E}$ is ordered by implication: $e_1 \succeq e_2$ iff e_2 logically implies e_1.

In Figure 3.1 we give an axiom scheme for two relations, $\approx$ and γ. The axioms for $\approx$ are a standard equational axiom scheme for Boolean algebra found in introductory textbooks (e.g., [11]). The relation γ (which is defined in terms of $\approx$) defines $\gamma(e_1)$ to be the set of all Boolean expressions e_2 such that $e_1 \vee e_2 \approx e_2$. Recall that we have defined $e_2 \succeq e_1$ iff e_1 logically implies e_2, i.e., $\neg e_1 \vee e_2$ is tautologically true. It is easy to see that γ and $\succeq$ are the same relation (slightly different ways of defining the same thing), and that $\gamma^* = \succeq$. But this simple refinement is not locally finite, since (for instance) $\gamma(x_1)$ contains x_1, $x_1 \vee x_1$, $x_1 \vee (x_1 \vee x_1)$, etc.

Note: In the axiom scheme below, defining the relations $\approx$ and γ, e_1, e_1', etc., represent arbitrary Boolean expressions.

Commutativity:	$e_1 \wedge e_2 \approx e_2 \wedge e_1$
	$e_1 \vee e_2 \approx e_2 \vee e_1$
Associativity:	$e_1 \wedge (e_2 \wedge e_3) \approx (e_1 \wedge e_2) \wedge e_3$
	$e_1 \vee (e_2 \vee e_3) \approx (e_1 \vee e_2) \vee e_3$
Absorption:	$e_1 \wedge (e_1 \vee e_2) \approx e_1$
	$e_1 \vee (e_1 \wedge e_2) \approx e_1$
Distributivity:	$e_1 \wedge (e_2 \vee e_3) \approx (e_1 \wedge e_2) \vee (e_1 \wedge e_3)$
	$e_1 \vee (e_2 \wedge e_3) \approx (e_1 \vee e_2) \wedge (e_1 \vee e_3)$
Bounds:	$e_1 \wedge \mathbf{false} \approx \mathbf{false}$
	$e_1 \vee \mathbf{true} \approx \mathbf{true}$
Complement:	$e_1 \wedge \neg e_1 \approx \mathbf{false}$
	$e_1 \vee \neg e_1 \approx \mathbf{true}$
Reflexivity:	$e_1 \approx e_1$
Symmetry:	if $(e_1 \approx e_2)$, then $(e_2 \approx e_1)$
Transitivity:	if $(e_1 \approx e_2)$ and $(e_2 \approx e_3)$, then $(e_1 \approx e_3)$
Substitution:	if $(e_1 \approx e_1')$, then: $(e_1 \wedge e_2) \approx (e_1' \wedge e_2)$,
	$\qquad\qquad\qquad (e_1 \vee e_2) \approx (e_1' \vee e_2)$, and
	$\qquad\qquad\qquad \neg e_1 \approx \neg e_1'$.
Generalization:	if $e_1 \vee e_2 \approx e_2$, then $(e_2, e_1) \in \gamma$.

Figure 3.1: Upward refinement axiom scheme for Boolean algebra.

Note: In the axiom scheme below, e_1, e_1', etc., are variables representing arbitrary Boolean expressions, while x_i indicates an arbitrary Boolean variable ($1 \leq i \leq n$). The relations are written in infix form: $\alpha \overset{\gamma}{\to} \beta$ means $(\beta, \alpha) \in \gamma_{\succeq}$, and $\alpha \overset{\approx}{\to} \beta$ means $(\beta, \alpha) \in \gamma_{\approx}$.

The relation γ':

$\gamma' = \gamma_{\approx} \cup \gamma_{\succeq}$.

The relation $\overset{\approx}{\to}$:

$e_1 \wedge e_2 \overset{\approx}{\to} e_2 \wedge e_1$ $\qquad\qquad\qquad\qquad$ $e_1 \vee e_2 \overset{\approx}{\to} e_2 \vee e_1$

$e_1 \wedge (e_2 \wedge e_3) \overset{\approx}{\to} (e_1 \wedge e_2) \wedge e_3$ $\qquad$ $e_1 \vee (e_2 \vee e_3) \overset{\approx}{\to} (e_1 \vee e_2) \vee e_3$

$e_1 \wedge (e_1 \vee \text{true}) \overset{\approx}{\to} e_1$ $\qquad\qquad\qquad$ $e_1 \vee (e_1 \wedge \text{false}) \overset{\approx}{\to} e_1$

$e_1 \wedge (e_1 \vee x_i) \overset{\approx}{\to} e_1$ $\qquad\qquad\qquad\quad$ $e_1 \vee (e_1 \wedge x_i) \overset{\approx}{\to} e_1$

$e_1 \wedge (e_1 \vee \text{false}) \overset{\approx}{\to} e_1$ $\qquad\qquad\quad$ $e_1 \vee (e_1 \wedge \text{true}) \overset{\approx}{\to} e_1$

$e_1 \wedge (e_2 \vee e_3) \overset{\approx}{\to} (e_1 \wedge e_2) \vee (e_1 \wedge e_3)$ $\quad$ $e_1 \vee (e_2 \wedge e_3) \overset{\approx}{\to} (e_1 \vee e_2) \wedge (e_1 \vee e_3)$

$\text{true} \wedge \text{false} \overset{\approx}{\to} \text{false}$ $\qquad\qquad\qquad$ $\text{true} \vee \text{true} \overset{\approx}{\to} \text{true}$

$\text{true} \wedge \text{true} \overset{\approx}{\to} \text{true}$ $\qquad\qquad\qquad\;$ $\text{false} \vee \text{false} \overset{\approx}{\to} \text{false}$

$x_i \wedge \text{false} \overset{\approx}{\to} \text{false}$ $\qquad\qquad\qquad\;$ $x_i \vee \text{true} \overset{\approx}{\to} \text{true}$

$\text{false} \wedge \text{false} \overset{\approx}{\to} \text{false}$ $\qquad\qquad\qquad$ $\text{false} \vee \text{true} \overset{\approx}{\to} \text{true}$

$\text{true} \wedge \neg\text{true} \overset{\approx}{\to} \text{false}$ $\qquad\qquad\quad\;$ $\text{true} \vee \neg\text{true} \overset{\approx}{\to} \text{true}$

$x_i \wedge \neg x_i \overset{\approx}{\to} \text{false}$ $\qquad\qquad\qquad\quad$ $x_i \vee \neg x_i \overset{\approx}{\to} \text{true}$

$\text{false} \wedge \neg\text{false} \overset{\approx}{\to} \text{false}$ $\qquad\qquad\;$ $\text{false} \vee \neg\text{false} \overset{\approx}{\to} \text{true}$

$\neg\text{true} \overset{\approx}{\to} \text{false}$ $\qquad\qquad\qquad\qquad$ $\neg\text{false} \overset{\approx}{\to} \text{true}$

if $e_1 \overset{\approx}{\to} e_1'$, then: $\quad e_1' \overset{\approx}{\to} e_1$ $\qquad\qquad$ $\neg e_1 \overset{\approx}{\to} \neg e_1'$

$\qquad\qquad\qquad\quad e_1 \wedge e_2 \overset{\approx}{\to} e_1' \wedge e_2$ $\qquad$ $e_1 \vee e_2 \overset{\approx}{\to} e_1' \vee e_2$

The relation $\overset{\gamma}{\to}$:

$x_i \overset{\gamma}{\to} \text{true}$ $\qquad\qquad\qquad\qquad\qquad$ $\text{false} \overset{\gamma}{\to} x_i$

if $e_1 \overset{\gamma}{\to} e_1'$, then:

$\qquad\qquad\qquad e_1 \wedge e_2 \overset{\gamma}{\to} e_1' \wedge e_2$

$\qquad\qquad\qquad e_1 \vee e_2 \overset{\gamma}{\to} e_1' \vee e_2$

$\qquad\qquad\qquad \neg e_1' \overset{\gamma}{\to} \neg e_1$

Figure 3.2: Locally finite upward refinement for Boolean algebra.

In Figure 3.2 another axiom scheme is given for the relation $\gamma' = \gamma_{\approx} \cup \gamma_{\succeq}$. One can show by induction that γ' is locally finite, by arguing that both $\gamma_{\approx}$ and $\gamma_{\succeq}$ are computable and finite. For example, $\gamma'(x_1)$ is $\{\text{true}, x_1 \vee (x_1 \wedge \text{true}), x_1 \vee (x_1 \wedge \text{false}), x_1 \wedge (x_1 \vee x_i), x_1 \vee (x_1 \wedge x_i), x_1 \wedge (x_1 \vee \text{false}), x_1 \vee (x_1 \wedge \text{true})\}$, where x_i ranges over X.

It may not be obvious that γ' is a refinement for $\succeq$, and so a sketch of the (tedious) proof that it is a locally finite refinement is included in the appendix to this chapter. However, one should note what was done to γ to make it locally finite. In particular, no steps of the form $\alpha \equiv \beta$ have been included unless every variable in α also occurs in β, and vice versa. Rules in Figure 3.1 where this condition does not hold have been replaced in Figure 3.2 by a set of rules in which the unmatched variable has been instantiated to true, false, and each of the symbols x_i. $\triangle$

Example 3.3 . The upward refinement γ for rationals described in 2.13 is not locally finite. We can, however, construct one that is, using the following fact: given $p_1 < p_2$ and $q_1 < q_2$, we can compute the set of ratios p/q such that $p_1 \leq p \leq p_2$ and $q_1 \leq q \leq q_2$. Combining this with the size idea above, we proceed as follows: Let $size(p) = \max[\lfloor \log_2 |p| \rfloor + 1, 1]$. (Thus $size(p)$ is the number of bits needed to represent p, irrespective of sign.) Then $\gamma(p/q)$ is essentially the set of all ratios p'/q' greater than p/q such that the sizes of p' and q' differ from those of p and q, resp., by at most one bit. Formally,

$$\gamma(p/q) \;=\; \{p'/q' \neq p/q \mid \quad p'q \geq q'p, \; |size(p') - size(p)| \leq 1,$$
$$\text{and } |size(q') - size(q)| \leq 1\}.$$

For example, for $p/q = 1/3$, $size(1) = 1$ and $size(3) = 2$; $\gamma(1/3)$ consists of all ratios $p'/q' \geq 1/3$ (except 1/3 itself) with $0 \leq |p| \leq 3$ and

$1 \leq |q| \leq 7$: $\{1/1, -1/-1, 2/1, -2/-1, \ldots, 3/7, -3/-7\}$.

$\triangle$

Definition 3.4 An expression $\bar{e} \in \mathcal{E}$ is said to be *minimal* if there is
no expression $e \in \mathcal{E}$ such that $h(\bar{e}) > h(e)$. A set $L \subseteq \mathcal{E}$ is said to be a
lower bounding set for $\mathcal{E}$ if, for every $e \in \mathcal{E}$, $h(e) \geq h(\bar{e})$ for some $\bar{e} \in L$

Dual definitions apply to *maximal* elements and *upper bounding sets*.

Bounding sets give the refinement algorithm a place to start, so
that it doesn't have to search for lower or upper bounds to the target.
When there is a (computable) finite bounding set L, and the refinement
is complete, we can initialize the search with the expressions in L and
be certain that we shall encounter a correct expression in $\gamma^*(L)$.

Example 3.5 For Boolean algebra, **true** is an upper bound, and **false**
a lower bound, for all expressions. There is no finite set of upper or
lower bounds for rationals. $\triangle$

The next definition is a slight extension of Definition 2.8. It states
when an ordering (or refinement) is semantically complete with respect
to a set of rules (instead of just a single rule).

Definition 3.6 For any subset L of $\mathcal{E}$, let $\mathcal{G}(L)$ be the set $\bigcup_{e \in L} \{e' \mid e' \succeq e\}$. The ordering $\succeq$ is said to be *semantically complete for* L if
$h(\mathcal{G}(L)) = \bigcup_{e \in L} \{d \mid d \geq h(e)\}$. If γ is a refinement for $\succeq$ and $\succeq$ is
semantically complete for L, then γ is likewise said to be semantically
complete for L.

The next algorithm modifies Algorithm 2.15 to take advantage of
a locally finite upward refinement complete for a finite set L of lower

bounds. The algorithm maintains a queue of possible rules, initially L. When the current hypothesis is refuted by a positive counterexample, it is generalized by computing its γ-related expressions, which are appended to the end of the queue. When the current hypothesis is refuted by a negative counterexample, it is simply discarded because generalizations are sure to be refuted by the same counterexample.

Algorithm 3.7 (Bottom-up Identification)

INPUT:

- A recursively enumerable set $\mathcal{E} = e_1, \ldots$, with a lower-bounding set $L = \bar{e}_1, \ldots, \bar{e}_s$.

- A locally finite, upward refinement γ, semantically complete for L.

- Oracles EX and $GE?$.

OUTPUT:

A sequence of expressions $H_1, H_2, \ldots$, such that H_i is correct for the first i examples.

PROCEDURE:

1. $H \leftarrow \bar{e}_1$. (Current hypothesis.)

2. $Q \leftarrow \bar{e}_2, \ldots, \bar{e}_s$. (Initialize Q.)

3. *examples* $\leftarrow$ *emptyset*.

4. Do forever:

   4.1 Add an example $EX()$ to *examples*.

   4.2 While H disagrees with some example:

4.21 If *too_specific*(H) and not *too_general*(H),

4.22 then add the expressions $\gamma(H)$ to Q.

4.23 $H \leftarrow next(Q)$.

4.3 Output H.

Note: Routines *too_general* and *too_specific* are given in Algorithm 2.15.   ◇

Theorem 3.8 Algorithm 3.7 identifies $\mathcal{E}$ in the limit.

PROOF: If some hypothesis H is never refuted by any counterexample, then H must be correct, since *EX* presents a sufficient set of examples. So the algorithm will neither converge to an incorrect hypothesis nor discard a correct one, and we need only show that it eventually finds a correct hypothesis.

From the completeness property of γ we know that there is a finite chain of refinement steps $r_0 \rightarrow \ldots \rightarrow r_n$, with $r_0 = \bar{e} \in L$, r_n representing d_0 (the target object), and $r_{i+1} \in \gamma(r_i)$, for $0 \leq i < n$. When $n = 0$ we have the trivial case where $h(\bar{e}) = d_0$. So assume n is greater than zero and as small as possible for the given d_0. The order-homomorphism property, together with the minimality of n, ensures that $r_0 \preceq \ldots \preceq r_n$ and that $h(r_i) \neq d_0$ for each $0 \leq i < n$. Thus for each r_i there is at least one positive example $+x_i$ such that $h(r_i) \not\preceq h(x_i)$; and for every negative example $-x$, $h(r_i) \not\preceq h(x)$ (for all $0 \leq i \leq n$).

We assume the algorithm diverges, and derive a contradiction. Below, we shall argue that divergence implies that r_n must become the hypothesis H at some point in the execution of the algorithm. Divergence also implies that every hypothesis is eventually discarded as a result of a counterexample. But r_n is correct for all examples and will never be discarded. Thus we are forced to conclude that the algorithm converges.

So assume that every hypothesis is eventually discarded. We argue, by induction on n, that r_n eventually becomes the hypothesis. r_0 is either the initial hypothesis or among the first $s - 1$ rules initially on the Q. Since by hypothesis all rules are eventually discarded, r_0 will become the current hypothesis. Suppose $H = r_i$, for $i < n$. Since we have argued that there exists a positive example x_i not covered by r_i, r_i will ultimately be discarded and its refinements added to the end of the Q. Q is always finite, since γ is locally finite. And since (by hypothesis) the algorithm diverges, the finite number of expression preceding r_{i+1} will all be tried as hypotheses and discarded. Thus r_{i+1} eventually becomes the current hypothesis.

From earlier comments, we conclude that the algorithm converges.

$\square$

The downward algorithm corresponding to 3.7 is entirely dual, obtained by replacing γ by ρ and the lower bounds by upper bounds. This duality is perhaps surprising, in view of the lack of duality between Algorithms 2.15 and 2.17. In fact, the duality is somewhat illusory, since the existence of a locally finite, complete upward refinement and a finite set of lower bounding elements does not imply the existence of the dual downward refinement and upper bounding elements. (For an OQI, however, this duality is actual.)

A third property that is useful for speeding up the identification process is that of *separability*. It is common for $\gamma(e)$ to include expressions that are h-equivalent to e. If we test e and find that it needs to be refined, it is silly to test its equivalents later as hypotheses. This does *not* mean, however, that we can simply discard the rules equivalent to e in $\gamma(e)$: doing so may void the completeness of the refinement. Provided we can recognize the equivalents, however, we can hold them on the queue, and when they reach the front, refine them without testing them against examples.

The formal property of the refinement that makes this possible is as follows.

Definition 3.9 A refinement γ is said to be *separable* if it can be decomposed into two relations, $\gamma_>$ and $\gamma_\approx$, such that

- $\gamma = \gamma_> \cup \gamma_\approx$.

- $\gamma_> \cap \gamma_\approx = \emptyset$.

- $\gamma_\approx \subseteq \approx$.

To express this more intuitively, a refinement is separable if we can generate separately the expressions in $\gamma(e)$ that are equivalent to e from those that are inequivalent. To compute $\gamma(e)$ for a separable refinement, we compute both $\gamma_>(e)$ and $\gamma_\approx(e)$ and take their union. Both sets of expressions will generally be needed to ensure that $\gamma^* = \succeq$. However, the algorithm can recognize those expressions equivalent to e, and handle them differently from those that are strict generalizations.

In practice, such a total separation may be hard to achieve, since it implies that the two subsets of expressions are both r.e. However, we can also make good use of a *partial* separation of γ into $\gamma_\geq$ and $\gamma_\approx$, where $\gamma_\approx \subseteq \approx$. ($\gamma_\geq$ and $\gamma_\approx$ may not be disjoint.)

Example 3.10 The refinement γ in Figure 3.1 is not separable as written. However, that in Figure 3.2 is partially separated by $\gamma_\geq$ and $\gamma_\approx$, since $\gamma_\approx$ generates strict equivalents, and $\gamma_\geq$ usually does not.

For the rational-numbers refinement in Example 3.3, it is easy to decide which ratios in $\gamma(p/q)$ are equivalent to p/q, and so this refinement can be strictly separated.

$\triangle$

Given a (partially) separable refinement, we should have no difficulty adapting an algorithm such as Algorithm 3.7 to use it by maintaining a flag identifying elements on the queue that were generated by $\gamma_\approx$. When these elements reach the front of the queue, they are not used as hypotheses; provided they still fail only on positive examples (as was the case when they were first enqueued), they are refined upward. The details are omitted.

3.3 Normal Forms and Monotonic Operations

When the algebra of the rule space $\mathcal{E}$ possesses a normal-form property, it may be possible to exploit it in the identification procedure. We may gain by searching over that subset of the rules that are in normal form. Also, understanding how the special syntactic form of the rule relates to its meaning may enable us to generalize only the parts that are too special.

For example, Shapiro and others have taken advantage of the conjunctive and disjunctive normal forms of logical sentences. Shapiro's algorithm [66] does not resemble Algorithm 3.7 for this very reason. The main result of this section is to demonstrate that the structure of his algorithm is not specific to logical domains, but instead results from the existence of an algebraic property — namely, the existence of a normal form for h-monotonic operations. As an application, we present an identification algorithm for a domain that has a disjunctive, but no conjunctive, normal form.

Definition 3.11 Let $\circ$ be a binary operation in the algebra $\mathcal{E}$ of expressions. We say that $\circ$ is h-*monotonic downward* if, for every pair e_1 and e_2 of expressions in $\mathcal{E}$, $h(e_i) \geq h(e_1 \circ e_2)$ (for $i = 1, 2$). Similarly, $\circ$ is h-*monotonic upward* if $h(e_1 \circ e_2) \geq h(e_i)$ (for $i = 1, 2$).

For consistency, we shall let $\odot$ represent an arbitrary h-monotonic downward operation on $\mathcal{E}$, and $\oplus$ an h-monotonic upward operation, throughout this section. We shall also assume that $\odot$ and $\oplus$ are associative and commutative.

Definition 3.12 An expression $e \in \mathcal{E}$ is said to be a $\odot$-*component* if the operation $\odot$ does not occur in e. Similarly, e is a $\oplus$-*component* if $\oplus$ does not occur in e.

Definition 3.13 $\mathcal{E}$ is said to have a $\odot$-*normal form property* if the following is true: for every semantic object $d \in \mathcal{D}$, there exists a finite set $\{e_1, \ldots, e_n\}$ of $\odot$-components such that $d = h(e_1 \odot \ldots \odot e_n)$.
A $\oplus$-*normal form property* is similarly defined, replacing $\odot$ by $\oplus$.

Example 3.14 Let $\mathcal{E}$ be the class of first-order sentences in a language $\mathcal{L}$, and $\mathcal{D}$ the class of Herbrand models. It is well known that every sentence in $\mathcal{E}$ can be written both in conjunctive and in disjunctive normal form (CNF and DNF). Logical disjunction is h-monotonic upward, for if $\mathcal{M}$ is a model of φ_1, then it is a model of $\varphi_1 \vee \varphi_2$ also. Similarly, logical conjunction is h-monotonic downward. $\triangle$

Example 3.15 Regular expressions have a "+"–normal form but no "·"–normal form. To see this, recall the identity $(R_1 + R_2)^* = (R_1^* R_2^*)^*$. This identity can be applied recursively to eliminate "+" operations from within a "*"–ed expression. Together with the fact that "·" distributes over "+", we can easily construct an algorithm to convert any regular expression to the form $R_1 + \ldots + R_n$, where no R_i contains the operation "+". $\triangle$

Definition 3.16 An expression e is said to be *too general* with respect to a target object d_0 if, for any expression e_0 such that $h(e_0) = d_0$, it is the case that $h(e_0 \oplus e) > d_0$. Similarly, e is said to be *too specific* for d_0 if $h(e_0 \odot e) < d_0$.

Let us now focus principally on the $\odot$ operation, with the understanding that dual statements apply to $\oplus$. We abbreviate "$\odot$-component" to "component".

Definition 3.17 We say that e is *correct for* d_0 if, for any e_0 representing d_0, $h(e \odot e_0) = d_0$.

The next result plays a central role in the normal-form identification algorithm. In essence it says that when an $\odot$-normal form expression is too specific, it is sufficient to generalize some of its components. We don't have to discard the whole expression.

Lemma 3.18 Let $e = e_1 \odot \ldots \odot e_n$ be a $\odot$-normal form expression, d_0 an object for which there exists an $\odot$-normal form expression, and $+x$ a positive example of d_0. If $h(e) \not\geq h(x)$, then there exists a component e_i of e that is too specific for d_0.

PROOF: Let e_0 be a $\odot$-normal form expression for d_0. If no component of e is too specific, then $e_0 \odot e_1$ is a normal form expression such that either $h(e_0 \odot e_1) \geq h(e_0)$, or $(e_0 \odot e_1)$ and e_0 are incomparable. But monotonicity of $\odot$ requires that $h(e_0 \odot e_1) \leq h(e_0)$; consequently, they cannot be incomparable, and it must follow that $e_0 \odot e_1$ is h-equivalent ($\approx$) to e_0. The same argument holds for e_2, using $e_0 \odot e_1$ as an expression for d_0, leading to the conclusion that $e_0 \odot e_1 \odot e_2$ is equivalent to e_0. And we can continue this, until we have shown that $e_0 \odot e$ and e_0 are h-equivalent. But now we have $h(x) \leq h(e_0) = h(e \odot e_0) \leq h(e)$ contradicting the assumption that $h(e) \not\geq h(x)$.

$\square$

Knowing that a normal-form expression includes at least one component that is too specific, how do we identify such a component? The obvious approach is test each component until one is found which fails to cover the positive example. This may not work, however, since in our model, $e_1 \odot e_2$ may be far more specific than either e_1 or e_2: there may be examples covered by both e_1 and e_2 alone but not by $e_1 \odot e_2$.

Dually, if $e_1 \oplus e_2$ is too general and $-x$ is a counterexample, then at least one of e_1 or e_2 is too general. However, it may be the case that neither e_1 nor e_2 alone covers the example, as the following illustrates.

Example 3.19 Shapiro's Model Inference System restricts $\mathcal{E}$ to be Horn sentences over a fixed first-order language. For such a sentence φ, Shapiro defines the meaning $h(\varphi)$ to be the set of Herbrand atoms implied by ϕ. For example, let p and q be predicate symbols in a first-order language $\mathcal{L}$ that also contains f as a function symbol and c as a constant. The sentence $\forall x\, p(x)$ has as its meaning the set of atoms $\{p(c), p(f(c)), p(f(f((c)))), \ldots\}$. Note that, for this domain, logical $\wedge$ is h-monotonic *upward*. (Compare Example 3.14.)

Suppose $\varphi_0 = \forall x\, p(x)$ represents the target model, but that our current hypothesis for the target is:

$$H = \forall x\, (p(x) \to q(x)) \wedge (p(f(c)))\,.$$

A negative counterexample to H is $q(f(c))$, since this is implied by H but not by φ_0.

However, consider the components of H: neither $p(f(c))$ nor $\forall x$ $(p(x) \to q(x))$ by itself implies $q(f(c))$. Thus the meaning of H is more than the "sum" of its parts.

$$\triangle$$

The task of finding a component that is too specific or too general in a hypothesis is called the *diagnosis problem*. For example, [66] presents an elegant algorithm for diagnosing Horn sentences. In general, the diagnosis task depends on the nature of the particular domain. In order to retain our domain-independent viewpoint, we shall assume an oracle *DIAGNOSE* that accepts a positive example and an expression that fails to cover that example, and returns a component of e that is too specific. Extending Shapiro's diagnosis algorithms to algebraic domains other than logic is seen as an interesting problem for further research.

The next definition extends Definition 3.4 to the case of normal-form expressions.

Definition 3.20 Let $\mathcal{E}$ have an $\odot$-normal form property. A component $\bar{e} \in \mathcal{E}$ is said to be *minimal* if there is no component $e \in \mathcal{E}$ such that $h(\bar{e}) > h(e)$. A set L of components is said to be a *lower bounding set* for $\mathcal{E}$ if $L \subseteq \mathcal{E}$ and, for every component $e \in \mathcal{E}$, $h(e) \geq h(\bar{e}_i)$ for some $\bar{e}_i \in L$.

The major advantage to working with normal forms is that the refinements can be restricted to components instead of to all expressions. Consequently the relations are simpler to construct and to work with. The next definition states what we mean by a component refinement.

Definition 3.21 Suppose $\mathcal{E}$ enjoys a $\odot$-normal form property. An r.e. binary relation γ is said to be an *upward refinement for components* if, for any component e, $\gamma^*(e) = \{e' \mid e' \text{ is a component, and } e' \succeq e\}$.

Let L be a set of lower bounding components. We say that γ is *semantically complete for* L if $h(\bigcup_{\bar{e} \in L} \gamma^*(\bar{e}))$ includes $h(e)$ for every component $e \in \mathcal{E}$.

We can now give an identification algorithm for $\odot$-normal-form expressions, using an upward refinement for components. We shall assume that γ is locally finite and complete for a finite set of lower bounding components.

Algorithm 3.22 (Upward Inference of $\odot$-Normal-Form Rules)

INPUT:

- An r.e. set of expressions $\mathcal{E}$ such that $\odot$ is h-monotonic upward and a $\odot$-normal form theorem applies.

- A finite set $L = \{\bar{e}_1, \ldots, \bar{e}_s\}$ of lower-bounding $\odot$-components.

- A locally finite, upward component refinement γ semantically complete for L.

- Oracles EX, $GE?$, and $DIAGNOSE$.

OUTPUT:

A sequence H_1, H_2, ... of $\odot$-normal form expressions such that H_i is correct for the first i examples.

PROCEDURE:

1. $H \leftarrow \bar{e}_1, \ldots, \bar{e}_s$. (The hypothesis is represented as a set of components, implicitly connected by $\odot$. Initially, H contains all minimal components.)

2. $Q \leftarrow emptyset$. (Initialize queue.)

3. $examples \leftarrow emptyset$. (Save examples)

4. Do forever:

   4.1 Get the next example from $EX()$ and add it to the set $examples$.

   4.2 While H disagrees with some example:

   4.21 If $GE?(H, x) = \text{false}$ for some positive example $+x$:

   4.211 Identify a component $e = DIAGNOSE(H, x)$ of H that is too specific.

   4.212 Remove e from H.

   4.213 Add $\gamma(e)$ to Q.

4.22 If $GE?(H, x) = $ **true** for some negative example $-x$:

   4.221 Remove a component e from the front of Q. (The algorithm fails if Q is empty).

   4.222 Add e to H.

4.3 Output H as the $\odot$ of each component in H.   ◇

The algorithm assumes, among other things, that γ is locally finite and complete for a finite lower-bounding set L of components. The hypothesis H is maintained as a set of components which are implicitly joined by $\odot$-operations. Initially H contains only the set L. A new example starts up a **while**-loop that keeps modifying H as long as it disagrees with some example in storage. If H is too specific (fails on a positive example), an oracle is invoked to pinpoint one of the components of H that is too specific. That component is evicted, and its upwardly refined forms are added to the queue. If H is too general, we make it less so by adjoining components to it. From the preceding discussion, we know that we cannot in general be very discriminating about what we add; in fact, the algorithm just grabs components as they occur on the queue until its requirement to cover a particular positive example has been satisfied. It appears there might be some risk that the queue could be exhausted before the example has been covered, but in the proof we show that this cannot happen. Eventually this process of grabbing new components, discarding and refining old ones ends with the hypothesis correct for all the examples, whereupon a new example is summoned, and the iteration begins again.

Theorem 3.23 Algorithm 3.22 identifies D in $\odot$-normal form, in the limit.

PROOF: Assume that the algorithm eventually reads in every example and converges to some hypothesis. Then it converges to a correct hypothesis, since the **while**-loop ensures that every positive example and no negative examples are covered. Thus we need to show that every example is eventually read – i.e., , that the **while**-loop terminates for every finite set of examples – and that the algorithm will not keep modifying the hypothesis forever.

Let d_0 be the target object, and let $e_0 = e_{01} \odot \cdots \odot e_{0k}$ be a normal-form expression for d_0. First, we claim that, *without loss of generality, we can assume that for each e_{0i} there is a refinement path from an element of L to e_{0i} along which e_{0i} is the only component that is not too specific.* Consider any component e_{0i} of e_0. Since γ is complete for L, e_{0i} (or some equivalent) is derivable from some component $\bar{e}$ in L by γ-refinement. Take any such sequence $\bar{e} = c_1 \xrightarrow{\gamma} \cdots \xrightarrow{\gamma} c_n \approx e_{0i}$ and determine the first component c_i in the chain which is *not* too specific for e_0. This is clearly possible since e_{0i} is not too specific. If c_i is not e_{0i} then we can replace e_{0i} by c_i in the expression $e_0 = e_{01}\odot\cdots\odot e_{0i}\odot\cdots\odot e_{0k}$ and obtain $e_0' = e_{01} \odot \cdots \odot c_i \cdots \odot e_{0k}$ as an equivalent expression for d_0. And by repeating this construction for each of the components of e_0, we obtain an expression $c_1 \odot \cdots \odot c_k$ for d_0 with the property that each component has a refinement path from a minimal element and that c_i is the first component on the path not too specific for d_0. Also, replacing c_i by any other component along the path yields an expression too specific for d_0. Thus the claim is proved.

Now let $e_0 = c_1 \odot \cdots \odot c_k$ be such an expression. Make the following observations:

1. Once a component c_i of e_0 is added to H, it will never be refined. (Only components that are too specific are refined).

2. Let $\bar{e} \xrightarrow{\gamma} \cdots \xrightarrow{\gamma} c_i$ be a refinement path from a minimal element $\bar{e}$ to c_i such that c_i is the only component in the path that is not too specific for d_0. Then at least one of the components on the path is always in either H or Q: Clearly this holds at the outset. c_i, once added, will never be removed; and the other components (being too specific) will be refined upon removal, with successor components added to the queue.

The **while**-loop can fail either by exhausting the queue during its attempt to satisfy a negative example, or by searching forever for a set H of components correct for some finite set of examples. *We claim that neither of these can occur.*

The second observation ensures that the queue cannot be exhausted; for among the components in H and Q there are always components as specific as c_i for each i. Thus the **while** loop will always be able to satisfy any negative example. No queue elements are disturbed when removing components from H in order to cover a positive example, and the first observation guarantees that the **while**-loop will not go too far in removing or refining a correct component. Thus for any finite set of examples, the **while**-loop will terminate successfully, proving the claim.

Assume now, for the sake of contradiction, that the algorithm never converges to a correct hypothesis. Because of the FIFO queuing discipline, every component in the refinement path from $\bar{e}$ to c_i (for each component c_i of e_0) will be added to H at some point, and discarded (and refined) once a positive example is presented for which the component is too specific. When all of the components of e_0 have been added to H, it is no longer possible that H will cover a negative example. Thereafter, the only possible changes to H are removal of components that are too specific. But since H is finite, only a finite number of such changes are possible, contradicting the assumption that H changes infinitely often. □

The algorithm for $\oplus$-normal form expressions, using an upper bounding set and a downward refinement for components, is completely dual. We illustrate its use in the next example.

Example 3.24 As noted earlier, any regular expression can be put into disjunctive (+) normal form using the identity $(\alpha + \beta)^* = (\alpha^* \beta^*)^*$. In particular, over the alphabet $\Sigma = \{\sigma_1, \ldots, \sigma_n\}$, the upper-bounding expression $(\sigma_1 + \ldots + \sigma_n)^*$ can be written in the form $\top = (\sigma_1^* \ldots \sigma_n^*)^*$. With a downward refinement ρ for components complete for $\top$, and a diagnosis procedure for determining whether a component represented by a given expression contains a given string, we can utilize (the dual of) Algorithm 3.22. The diagnosis procedure is well known (e.g., , [1]).

A refinement is as follows. (E, E_1, etc. denote any regular expression not containing +. $\alpha \overset{\rho}{\to} \beta$ indicates that $\beta \in \rho(\alpha)$.)

$$\mathsf{T} \overset{\rho}{\to} (\mathsf{T} \cdot \mathsf{T})$$
$$\mathsf{T} \overset{\rho}{\to} (\mathsf{T}^*)$$
$$E^* \overset{\rho}{\to} (E \cdot E^*)$$
$$\sigma_i \overset{\rho}{\to} \phi \;(\text{for } 1 \leq i \leq n)$$

If $E_1 \overset{\rho}{\to} E$, then: $E_1^* \overset{\rho}{\to} E^*$

$$E_1 \cdot E_2 \overset{\rho}{\to} E \cdot E_2$$
$$E_2 \cdot E_1 \overset{\rho}{\to} E_2 \cdot E.$$

It is straightforward to verify that $\rho^*(\mathsf{T})$ includes every $+$-free regular expression, so that ρ is complete for T. $\triangle$

In conclusion, we have shown how a normal-form property over monotonic operations can be exploited in refinement algorithms. The algorithms above are very close in structure to the identification algorithm used in Shapiro's Model Inference System – further evidence that the success of his techniques depend very little on first-order logic but apply more generally to domains with an appropriate normal form.

We should also note the apparent asymmetry that arises when a domain possesses a $\odot$-normal form but not a $\oplus$-normal form (or dually): for our algorithms, the upward (resp., downward) direction is easier to handle than the downward (resp., downward). One is led to ask whether equally efficient algorithms for the opposite direction (e.g., upward for the case of regular expressions) might be found.

3.4   Universal Refinements

We have seen that there are many possible refinements for any given domain. In practice tuning the operators to the particular identification task is sure to be an important step in any application. For example, Shapiro achieved quite respectable timings largely through this process of carefully tuning the refinement. We are naturally led to ask what structure the class of refinement operators for a domain might have. Furthermore, since a refinement operator determines what rules will be considered as hypotheses, and since its implementation determines in what order those rules will be considered, the choice of a refinement operator closely parallels the choice of an *inductive bias* ([47] and [69]).

This section explores these ideas in more detail. The aims are (1) to provide a theoretical basis for the concept of inductive bias, and (2) to show that in some sense refinement can be viewed as a specialized model of computation.

3.4.1 Abstract Formulation

First we shall describe universal refinements abstractly in terms of relations and sub-relations. Subsequently, we shall construct a universal refinement for the particular domain of clause-form predicate logic.

Although the fundamental ideas in this section are not difficult, they are difficult to explain. I apologize in advance for the relatively turbid presentation to follow.

Let $\mathcal{E}$ and $\mathcal{D}$ be fixed; assume also that an ordering $\succeq_1$ and a refinement γ_1 for that ordering have been developed. These relations determine which generalizations or specializations of a hypothesis may be tested during the identification procedure. In particular, if $\succeq_1$ and γ_1 are complete, then a semantically complete set of generalizations can be tested.

But this set may be larger than necessary. For example, we have seen refinements for which $\gamma_1^*(e)$ eventually generates every possible rule more general than e, including all equivalents of each rule. Also, it may be possible to do without a semantically complete set if other circumstances (e.g., prior experience) indicate that certain types of rules need not be considered. Under these conditions, a smaller ordering $\succeq_2$, and a corresponding refinement γ_2, may be more expeditious. So we are motivated to define sub-refinements and extend the "more/less general than" relations to refinements themselves.

Definition 3.25 Let $\succeq_1$ be an ordering for $\mathcal{E}$ and γ_1 a refinement for $\succeq_1$. We say that the relation γ_2 is *less general than* γ_1 if $\gamma_2 \subseteq \succeq_1$. Correspondingly, we say that the ordering $\succeq_2 = \gamma_2^*$ is less general than $\succeq_1$.

Note that γ_2 is less general than γ_1 iff $\succeq_2 \subseteq \succeq_1$. Also, γ_2 is necessarily an order-preserving relation, since it is a subset of $\succeq_1$.

In choosing a less-general refinement than γ_1, we might envision an operator $\hat{\rho}$ that enumerates all refinements γ_2 less general than γ_1. Such an operator itself feels like a refinement — a refinement on a domain of refinements, instead of on $\mathcal{E}$. In order to describe $\hat{\rho}$ as a refinement, we need to establish the domain over which it is defined, a domain which will be parameterized by $\mathcal{E}$.

SEMANTICS: Let $\mathcal{D}_1$ be the class of r.e. binary relations over $\mathcal{E}$. (Such relations are, of course, sets of pairs of rules in $\mathcal{E}$.) The partial ordering of $\mathcal{D}_1$ is $\subseteq$ (set containment).

> SYNTAX: Let $\mathcal{E}_1$ be some r.e. representation for binary rela-
> tions on $\mathcal{E}$. (In the next subsection, we shall use pred-
> icate calculus as the representation, but the relations
> could also be expressed in LISP, as Turing machines,
> etc.) If γ_1 is a semantically complete refinement for $\mathcal{E}$,
> then we can treat γ_1 as the upper bound for the class
> of relations we are interested in.
>
> MAPPING: Let γ be any expression in $\mathcal{E}_1$. $h(\gamma)$ is the set of
> pairs (e_1, e_2) in $\mathcal{E} \times \mathcal{E}$ such that $e_1 \in \gamma(e_2)$.

The goal is to obtain a complete refinement $\hat{\rho}$ – i.e., , a binary relation $\hat{\rho}$ over $\mathcal{E}_1$ such that $\hat{\rho}^*(\gamma_1)$ includes some representation for every γ_2 less general than γ_1.

A way to obtain such a $\hat{\rho}$ is as follows. Let R be *any* r.e. binary relation on $\mathcal{E} \times \mathcal{E}$, and suppose that γ_1 is a refinement relation over $\mathcal{E}$. (Both R and γ_1 are elements of $\mathcal{D}_1$.) Then $\gamma_1^* \cap R$ is a sub-refinement of γ_1:

- $\gamma_1^* \cap R$ is an r.e. set, since γ_1 and R are, and r.e. sets are closed under intersection and *.

- Clearly, $(\gamma_1^* \cap R) \subseteq \gamma_1^*$, and hence satisfies the definition of a sub-refinement of γ_1.

Furthermore, every subrefinement γ_2 is $\gamma_1^* \cap R$ for some R, since $\gamma_2 = \gamma_1^* \cap \gamma_2$. Thus, *starting from a most general refinement γ_1 and construct-ing $\gamma_1 \cap R$ for every R, we shall obtain all subrefinements of γ_1.*

We now consider a binary relation $\hat{\rho}$ on $\mathcal{E}_1$ such that

1. if $R \in \hat{\rho}(\gamma_1)$, then the relation R is a subset of γ_1^*; and

LANGUAGE	PREDICATES	FUNCTIONS	CONSTANTS	VARIABLES
$\mathcal{L}$	p_1, p_2	f	c	$X, Y, \ldots$
$\mathcal{L}^{(1)}$	gamma, disjoint-vars, isa-atom, isa-term, ...	p_1, p_2, f, $\wedge$, $\vee$, $\neg$, ...	$c, X, Y, \ldots$	$X^{(1)}$, $Y^{(1)}$, ...
$\mathcal{L}^{(2)}$	disjoint-vars, isa-atom, isa-term ...	disjoint-vars, isa-atom, isa-term, p_1, p_2, f, $\wedge$, $\vee$, $\neg$, ...	c, X, Y, $X^{(1)}$, $Y^{(1)}$, ...	$X^{(2)}$, $Y^{(2)}$, ...

Figure 3.3: Languages used in constructing a universal refinement

2. $\hat{\rho}^*(\gamma_1)$ includes every subrelation of γ_1^*.

A relation $\hat{\rho}$ with these properties will be called a downward *universal refinement* relation. Definitions for an upward universal refinement, $\hat{\gamma}$, can also be given in the obvious way.

3.4.2   A Refinement for Clause-Form Sentences

We now choose a particular representation language for the syntax denoted above by $\mathcal{E}_1$, namely, the class of clause-form sentences in a first-order language. The table in Figure 3.3 may help in following the argument. Also, refer to the Appendix of this chapter for a summary of our logical terminology and notation.

A *clause-form sentence* in a first-order language $\mathcal{L}$ is a sentence over the symbols of $\mathcal{L}$ in the form $C_1 \wedge \ldots \wedge C_n$, where each C_i is a clause in prenex form with only universal quantification:

$$\forall x_1 \ldots \forall x_k [\ell_1 \vee \ldots \vee \ell_m],$$

where the ℓ_i's are atomic literals, and $x_1, \ldots, x_k$ are the distinct variables occurring in the ℓ_i's. We shall henceforth adopt the common notational convention that all variables in a clause are assumed to be universally quantified by a prenex quantifier $\forall$. The clause with no literals is indicated by $\square$ and is unsatisfiable. The sentence with no clauses is indicated by $\emptyset$ and is irrefutable.

Clause form is an expressive subclass of first-order sentences in that for any sentence there is an effective transformation to a clause-form sentence (perhaps in an expanded language) that is satisfiable iff the original sentence is satisfiable. A clause-form sentence for which each clause has at most one positive literal is said to be in Horn form. (Horn sentences form the basis of logic programming.)

Our proof system for clause-form logic is Resolution [58]. A sentence φ is unsatisfiable iff $\square$ can be derived from φ by repeatedly applying the resolution rule. We prove that $\varphi \vdash \psi$ by showing that $(\varphi \wedge \neg \psi) \vdash \square$.

A Representation for Refinements. In resolution proofs, the clauses may be non-deterministically selected in any order for computing resolvents. Thus representing a refinement as a clause-form sentence defines the relation without specifying any particular enumeration of the relation. What does a clause-form refinement look like? Let us assume that the language $\mathcal{L}$ in which the expressions $\mathcal{E}$ are written has a non-empty set of predicate symbols $p_1, p_2, \ldots$, a (possibly empty) set of function symbols $f_1, \ldots$, and a non-empty set of constant symbols $c_1, \ldots$.

Let us try to describe a typical language $\mathcal{L}^{(1)}$ for defining refinement relations γ over $\mathcal{L}$, without getting into too many details. There will be a two-place predicate *gamma* such that the set of instantiations of the variable X which satisfy $gamma(X, e)$ is precisely the set $\gamma(e)$. The definition of *gamma* will in turn depend upon other predicates, such as those needed to define the syntactic form of a sentence in $\mathcal{L}$: for example, *has-literal*(X, Y), which is satisfied iff X is a literal in the formula Y, and *enlarges-clause*(C_1, L, C_2), which is satisfied iff adding the literal L to the clause C_1 yields the clause C_2.

The predicates and function symbols in $\mathcal{L}$, along with the logical operations $\neg$, $\vee$, and $\wedge$, will appear as function symbols in the language $\mathcal{L}^{(1)}$ used to define *gamma*. For example, assume that p is a predicate symbol in $\mathcal{L}$. A predicate *isa-atom* in $\mathcal{L}^{(1)}$, expressing the fact that X is a well-formed atom, might include, among others, the clause: "if $X = p(X_1)$ and *isa-term*(X_1) then *isa-atom*(X)". In this non-standard syntax, X and X_1 are variables, "$=$", "*isa-atom*" and "*isa-term*" are predicates, and "p" serves (here) as a function symbol.

To summarize, the language in which *gamma* is defined is a language $\mathcal{L}^{(1)}$ quite different from $\mathcal{L}$, and related to the latter only in that the symbols of $\mathcal{L}$ are included as function and constant symbols in $\mathcal{L}^{(1)}$. For specific examples of refinements, expressed in Prolog, see Shapiro's dissertation [66].

Assume now that we have in fact expressed *gamma* as a clause-form sentence over $\mathcal{L}^{(1)}$. Recall that we are really interested in universal refinements: we want to be able to refine this sentence (and others like it) so as to make it more specific. Therefore we shall require a refinement for clause-form sentences – specifically, a downward refinement which operates on a complete refinement like *gamma* to make it more specific. Before doing this, however, we need to be clear about the domain and its ordering.

Let $\mathcal{E}$ be the class of clause-form sentence over $\mathcal{L}$. Order $\mathcal{E}$ by implication: $\varphi_1 \succeq \varphi_2$ if $\varphi_1 \vdash \varphi_2$. Note that $\square$ is an upper bound for $\langle \mathcal{E}, \succeq \rangle$ since $\square \vdash \varphi$ for all φ; likewise $\emptyset$ is a lower bound. For semantics we take $\mathcal{D}$ to be sets of ground (i.e., variable-free) clauses, partially ordered by $\supseteq$:

$$h(\varphi) = \{C \mid C \text{ is a ground clause and } \varphi \vdash C\}.$$

We shall require the following easy, but useful, result.

Lemma 3.26 h is an OQI between $\langle \mathcal{E}, \succeq \rangle$ and $\langle \mathcal{D}, \supseteq \rangle$.

PROOF: First assume that φ_1 and φ_2 are clause-form sentences such that $\varphi_2 \vdash \varphi_1$. Then if $C \in h(\varphi_1)$, we have $\varphi_2 \vdash (\varphi_1 \to C)$, and so $\varphi_2 \vdash C$. Thus $h(\varphi_2) \supseteq h(\varphi_1)$.

In the other direction, let S_1 and S_2 be sets of ground clauses, with $S_1 \subseteq S_2$. Also, for $i = 1, 2$ let $h(\varphi_i) = S_i$. We claim that $\varphi_2 \vdash \varphi_1$. For, suppose otherwise. φ_1 is in clause form, so we can write $\varphi_1 = (\forall \bar{e} C_1) \wedge \cdots \wedge (\forall \bar{e} C_n)$ ($\bar{e}$ generically indicates all the quantified variables). Let M be a model in which φ_2 is true but not φ_1. Then some clause $\forall \bar{e} C_i$ is false in M. If C_i explicitly contains any of the variables $\bar{e}$, then there is a ground instance C_i^0 of C_i which is false in M; else, C_i is a ground clause, and we take $C_i^0 = C_i$. In either case, $\varphi_1 \vdash C_i^0$. Clearly $\varphi_2 \nvdash C_i^0$, since then M would verify C_i^0. But with C_i^0 we have a counterexample to the assumption that $S_1 \subseteq S_2$. The completes the proof. $\square$

We shall compose a downward refinement for clause-form sentences in two stages. First, we present a relation ρ_c on clauses with the property that $\rho_c^*(\square)$ is a set of clauses that includes at least one variant[1] of every clause. This relation is then used as part of the general refinement for clause-form sentences.

For notational efficiency, we shall use expressions such as

$$\beta_1, \ldots, \beta_n \rightarrow \alpha_1, \ldots, \alpha_p$$

to mean

$$\neg\beta_1 \vee \ldots \vee \neg\beta_n \vee \alpha_1 \vee \ldots \vee \alpha_p.$$

All variables in a clause are assumed to be universally quantified, unless overridden by explicit quantification. For the given language $\mathcal{L}$, the set of *most-general terms* consists of the constants and all terms of the form $f(x_1, \ldots, x_n)$, where f is an n-place function symbol $(n > 0)$ and the x_i are variables. The set of *most-general literals* consists of all literals of the form $p(x_1, \ldots, x_n)$ and $\neg p(x_1, \ldots, x_n)$, where p is an n-place predicate symbol $(n \geq 0)$.

Clause Refinement:

Definition 3.27 Let

$$\kappa = \beta_1, \ldots, \beta_n \rightarrow \alpha_1, \ldots, \alpha_p$$

$(n \geq 0, p \geq 0)$ be a clause in the language $\mathcal{L}$. $\rho_c(\kappa)$ is the set of clauses in $\mathcal{L}$ derived from κ by exactly one of the following operations:

---

[1] Clause C_1 is a *variant* of clause C_2 if they differ only in the naming of variables and the ordering and duplication of literals. Thus $p(f(x)) \vee q(y)$ is a variant of $p(f(x)) \vee q(x) \vee p(f(x))$. Variants have the same meaning.

$\rho_c(1)$:   Unifying two distinct variables x and y occurring in κ (i.e., replacing all occurrences of y in κ by x).

$\rho_c(2)$:   Substituting for all occurrences of a variable x occurring in κ most-general term t such that no variable in t occurs elsewhere in κ.

$\rho_c(3)$:   Disjoining a most-general literal, α_{p+1} or $\neg\beta_{n+1}$, to κ, such that no variable in the new literal occurs elsewhere in κ.

Example 3.28 Let $\kappa = p(f(x_1), y_1) \rightarrow p(x_1, f(y_1))$. In a language $\mathcal{L}$ that also includes a two-place function symbol g and a one-place predicate symbol q, $\rho_c(\kappa)$ includes the clauses:

$$p(f(x_1), x_1) \rightarrow p(x_1, f(x_1))$$

$$p(f(g(x_2, y_2)), y_1) \rightarrow p(g(x_2, y_2), f(y_1))$$

$$p(f(x_1), y_1) \rightarrow p(x_1, f(y_1)), q(x_2)$$

$$p(f(x_1), y_1), q(x_2) \rightarrow p(x_1, f(y_1))$$

$\triangle$

Lemma 3.29 (Shapiro) Over the language $\mathcal{L}$, ρ_c satisfies the following "completeness" property: for any clause κ in $\mathcal{L}$, there is a clause κ' in $\rho_c^*(\square)$ such that κ' is a variant of κ.

(This is just Theorem 5.14 from [65], expressed in our own notation.)

An implementation of ρ_c can treat variants of a clause as identical, and avoid generating variants of the same clause in computing $\rho_c(\kappa)$. Then ρ_c becomes locally finite.

Clause-form Sentence Refinement:

Definition 3.30 Let $\varphi = \kappa_1 \wedge \ldots \wedge \kappa_r$ be a clause-form sentence in the language $\mathcal{L}$, such that no variable occurs in more than one clause. The set $\hat{\rho}(\varphi)$ is the set of clause-form sentences derived from φ by exactly one of the following operations:

$\hat{\rho}(1)$:   Deleting a clause κ_i.

$\hat{\rho}(2)$:   Conjoining a new clause κ_{r+1} (with new variables) which is a most-general resolvent of two (not necessarily distinct) clauses in φ.

$\hat{\rho}(3)$:   Conjoining a new clause κ_{r+1} (with new variables) which is in $\rho_c(\kappa_i)$ for some $1 \leq i \leq r$.

Example 3.31 Let φ be the conjunction of the following two clauses:

$$\kappa_1 : \quad q(x_1) \rightarrow p(f(x_1))$$
$$\kappa_2 : \quad p(f(f(c))), q(g(y_1)) \rightarrow .$$

Then $\hat{\rho}(\varphi)$ includes the sentences κ_1, κ_2, $\kappa_1 \wedge \kappa_2 \wedge \kappa_3$, and $\kappa_1 \wedge \kappa_2 \wedge \kappa_4$, where

$$\kappa_3 : \quad q(f(c)), q(g(y_2)) \rightarrow$$
$$\kappa_4 : \quad p(f(f(c))), q(g(c)) \rightarrow .$$

κ_3 is obtained by unifying $p(f(x_1))$ in κ_1 with $p(f(f(c)))$ in κ_2 and resolving. Note that we rename the variables so that each clause has a disjoint set of variable names. κ_4 is obtained from κ_2 by substituting the most-general term c for the variable y_1. △

It is not difficult to check that $\hat{\rho}$ is locally finite. It is partially separable if we note that $\hat{\rho}(2)$ and $\hat{\rho}(3)$ yield equivalent sentences, while $\hat{\rho}(1)$ generally does not.

Main Result. We can now give the main result, namely that $\hat{\rho}$ is the universal downward refinement we are seeking.

Theorem 3.32 $\hat{\rho}$ is a downward refinement for the class of clause-form sentences over $\mathcal{L}$.

PROOF: The proof is lengthy, and is give in the appendix to this chapter. □

Corollary 3.33 $\hat{\rho}$ is semantically complete. Furthermore, the upward refinement $\gamma = \hat{\rho}^{-1}$ is also semantically complete.

PROOF: Immediate from Lemmas 2.14 and 3.29. □

Discussion. The proof of Theorem 3.32 has two parts: to show that, if $\varphi_2 \in \hat{\rho}(\varphi_1)$, then $\varphi_1 \succeq \varphi_2$; and to show that, if $h(\varphi_2) \subseteq h(\varphi_1)$, then φ_2 (or some equivalent) is in $\hat{\rho}^*(\varphi_1)$.

The first part shows that the steps of $\hat{\rho}$ result only in consequences of φ_1 – i.e., , *soundness*. The second part shows that some syntactic equivalent of every consequence will be generated – i.e., a form of *completeness.* In sum, $\hat{\rho}$ *is a proof system, modulo h-equivalence, for clause-form sentences.* The nature of the universality of $\hat{\rho}$ is now clear[2].

The upward refinement $\hat{\rho}^{-1}$ is not very useful. For example, the inverse of $\hat{\rho}(1)$ is to add an arbitrary clause. One can construct better upward refinements for clause-form sentences; but the problem of constructing a locally finite one is apparently open, and without this property the usefulness is questionable.

Ishizaka [35] attempts to overcome the problems of upward generalization by computing the least generalization of a set of ground atoms (examples) using Plotkin's algorithm [51]. He proposes an algorithm along the lines of Algorithm 3.7 for Prolog programs. However the algorithm is currently limited to programs with a bounded number of clauses for any given "head" (positive atom in a Horn clause).

Thus we encounter another situation for which refining in one direction is apparently easier than in the other. It may be that for a different domain the preferred direction is be upward, rather than downward, suggesting that the choice of domain (representation) can influence the nature of the algorithms for identification by refinement.

3.4.3   Inductive Bias

We now explore the following idea. If γ is a refinement over $\mathcal{E}$ that is represented in the domain $\mathcal{E}_1$, and if $\hat{\rho}$ is a complete refinement for expressions in $\mathcal{E}_1$, then $\hat{\rho}^*(\gamma)$ is a set of refinement-like relations that are

---

[2]It is *not* a complete proof system in the Hilbert sense because $\rho^*(\varphi)$ may not include all consequences of φ.

less general than γ. In particular, since ρ is complete, *every* such relation is included in the set $\rho^*(\gamma)$. And with some positive and negative feedback on how suitable a given refinement γ is, we could in principle search for a more suitable refinement γ', using the identification algorithms already presented. In a sense, we would be tuning the learning algorithm in response to its performance.

This general idea has already been proposed within the machine-learning community. Mitchell [47] suggested biasing the generalization process in favor of certain rules over others. In his thesis [69], Utgoff studied in depth the problem of adapting the class of admissible hypotheses to the performance of the learning algorithm, within a version-space context. The term *inductive bias* is used to describe the way in which rules are selected for evaluation as possible hypotheses. A *strong* bias is one in which only a small subset of $\mathcal{E}$ is considered, whereas a *weak* bias admits a larger class of rules. Obviously, if the bias is too strong, there may not be a suitable rule in the subset, and it will be necessary to weaken (i.e., generalize) the bias. The specific techniques for doing this are an important part of Utgoff's work, but for our purposes we may make the following suggestion: If we represent the bias by a refinement relation ς which generates only a subset of the possible rules in $\mathcal{E}$, then applying an upward refinement $\hat{\gamma}$ to ς can produce a refinement ς' with a weaker bias. In the reverse direction, a bias that is too weak may require excessive time to locate a hypothesis consistent with the examples; applying a downward refinement $\hat{\rho}$ can strengthen the bias and lead to faster convergence.

Let us be somewhat more specific. Call a relation γ a *partial upward refinement* provided, for all e_1, e_2 in $\mathcal{E}$ such that $e_2 \in \gamma(e_1)$, we have

$h(e_2) \geq h(e_1)$. A similar definition holds for partial downward refinements. Such a relation is partial in the sense that γ^* is not necessarily $\succeq$, the complete ordering on $\mathcal{E}$. In fact, the empty and the identity relations are both partial upward and downward refinements for any ordering $\succeq$. With a strong bias, we may not care whether γ^* covers the entire relation $\succeq$. Or, equivalently, the bias may have the effect of changing the ordering relation $\succeq$ on $\mathcal{E}$, a stronger bias corresponding to a sparser ordering relation.

Suppose now that γ is a partial refinement over $\mathcal{E}$, expressed in $\mathcal{E}_1$, and that $\hat{\rho}$ is a complete downward refinement for expressions in $\mathcal{E}_1$. Then every $\gamma' \in \hat{\rho}(\gamma)$ is a partial refinement over $\mathcal{E}$, with a bias as strong as or stronger than that of γ. Conversely, every downward refinement expressible in $\mathcal{E}_1$, with a bias stronger than that of γ, is in $\hat{\rho}^*(\gamma)$.

But we probably are not interested in generating *all* refinements with stronger or weaker biases. Utgoff, for example, applied heuristic rules for adjusting the bias; and Rendell [56] is exploring techniques for learning in a system with a variable bias. In our interpretation, the universal refinement $\hat{\rho}$ can itself be encoded in a language, say $\mathcal{E}_2$, and a universal refinement $\hat{\hat{\rho}}$ applied to it in order to strengthen the bias of the universal refinement which changes the bias. And in principle this hierarchy of universal refinements can be continued to more depths.

Utgoff observes that bias arises in other ways besides restricting the rules to a subset of $\mathcal{E}$. At any moment in executing an identification algorithm, there is a finite set of examples, and many rules consistent with the examples. Of all the possible consistent rules, only one is selected as the current guess, and so there is a bias in the way we select this one rule. How do we interpret this for refinement algorithms? Encoded as a logical sentence, a refinement γ is a non-deterministic program for computing $\gamma(e)$. Implementing this program on a real machine requires that determinism be imposed, and that the expressions in $\gamma(e)$ be generated in some specified order. Thus bias also arises from the manner in which the refinement is implemented.

Another type of bias comes from fixing the language in which the rules are expressed. For example, if our refinement generates regular expressions over an alphabet Σ, and we enlarge the alphabet, then we weaken the bias by admitting a whole new class of expressions. This type of bias is outside the scope of this theory, since we have assumed a fixed algebraic domain $\mathcal{E}$ and corresponding model $\mathcal{D}$ as a basis for all our results. And yet, in some sense, the task of determining the appropriate representation language for our rules is a major part of the inductive learning process. As noted before, how a domain is selected is a major, largely unexplored, aspect of the identification problem.

3.5   Conclusions

Let us try to draw some general conclusions from the many ideas introduced in this chapter.

Refinements as Programs. The main observation is that *to construct a refinement is to write a program.* The refinement program is a non-deterministic search program that starts from some expression e and follows a path of generalization or specialization steps in order to find another expression e'. The nondeterministic nature of the refinement makes it easier to design and test. We *verify* that it is in fact a refinement by showing that for every possible step $e_1 \to e_2$ of the refinement, $h(e_1) \geq h(e_2)$, and that it is sufficiently complete. Like other programming tasks, the refinement becomes more complex to construct and verify as further requirements (locally finite, separable, etc.) are imposed. And in common with other programming systems, there is a universal refinement program capable of refining itself as well as other refinement programs.

The refinement contains within it the *search* aspects of the identification problem. The algorithm that utilizes the refinement handles the bookkeeping aspects of the search – selecting examples, testing hypotheses, etc. Refinement algorithms are easier to understand and prove correct because they separate the search problem from the bookkeeping details.

While developing the ideas for this chapter, I constructed refinements for some of the domains described in the experimental AI literature (to the extent that they are specified in the literature). A good example is the *annotated predicate calculus* (APC) language of Michalski [45], which is clearly defined. The language includes extensions to standard predicate calculus syntax, such as a typed term algebra, counting and range quantifiers ("there exist between 3 and 8 values of x such that $\dots p(x) \dots$"), and *both... and, either... or,* and symmetric difference operations (e.g., $P(both\ t_1\ and\ t_2)$, meaning $P(t_1)\ and\ P(t_2)$) It also imposes restrictions on the form that formulas may take, so that the complexity of the formulas is quite limited. Evidently the syntax has been chosen as a compromise between the expressive power of the rules and the efficiency of the search. After a fair amount of work, I managed to construct what appeared to be a reasonable upward refinement for a subset of APC. I then tested it on several of the examples given in the paper; after discovering some bugs, I revised the refinement. Then, faced with the next step of proving that it was indeed a good refinement, I realized I was stuck: there is no good proof system for the APC. True, it is possible to translate any APC formula into standard predicate calculus, but in so doing we lose the ability to prove syntactical properties. (It is like trying to prove properties of a C program by first translating it to Fortran.)

The lesson to be drawn is a familiar one: in selecting a domain (representation) for an identification problem, we can choose an elaborate, special-purpose language without a simple, direct mapping h to its semantics, or we can choose a smaller, more restrictive language with a simpler, better understood semantics. Quite the same tradeoffs are involved when one chooses a rich programming language such as ADA or PL/I over a functional or logic-programming language: the former are more convenient for certain complex programming tasks, but the latter are much better for reasoning about the programs.

Refinements and Inductive Bias. The design of a refinement, and its implementation on a sequential machine, determine the inductive bias of the identification algorithm. The fact that refinements can themselves be refined (made more general or more specific) suggests that the process of learning an inductive bias, in the sense of Utgoff, is itself a problem of identification by refinement.

Weaknesses of the Refinement Approach. The theory offered so far is quite general in that it assumes relatively little about the domain, while characterizing many features of identification-by-refinement algorithms and supplying a firm foundation for studying these properties. But its generality is also its weakness, for it is probably too general to yield efficient algorithms directly or to suggest a useful measure of complexity.

Let us list some other limitations of the refinement-based induction approach:

- Refinement algorithms are still fundamentally enumerative. I know of no finite domain for which a refinement algorithm offers more than a polynomial speedup in the worst case over pure Identification by Enumeration. Unless a very strong bias can be adopted – whether by choice or by induction – refinement algorithms will probably perform poorly for at least some identification problems. The use of probability, as presented in Chapter 4, is a promising alternative, however.

- For identification in the limit, refinement algorithms tend to require that large numbers of examples and rules be kept in memory. In fact the storage requirements are often as big a limitation in these types of learning systems as the computation time. By contrast, other identification criteria may not suffer from this problem. (See, for example, Algorithm 4.2, as well as [26] and [63]).

- Refinement algorithms are highly sensitive to errors in the training examples. In all the algorithms we have presented so far, incorrect examples can cause a hypothesis to be irrevocably discarded, possibly along with all of its refined generalizations/specializations, in such a way that convergence is no longer possible. Rectifying this deficiency is the subject of Chapter 5.

- The need to fix the domain $(\mathcal{E}, \mathcal{D})$ in advance causes one to ask whether the domain itself could be inferred or at least enhanced [10]. This is a major open problem in inductive learning.

Despite these weaknesses, the theory does accomplish what is perhaps the major goal of this work: to extract a mathematical unity from diverse experimental results.

3.6 Appendix to Chapter 3

3.6.1 Summary of Logic Notation and Terminology

The purpose of this appendix is to summarize the notation and terminology used in this chapter. (It is *not* intended to be a tutorial.)

Let $\mathcal{L}$ be a given first-order language, consisting of a set of one or more predicate symbols $p_1, p_2, \ldots$, zero or more function symbols $f_1, \ldots$, and one or more constant symbols $c_1, \ldots$. Each symbol also has a fixed arity; constant symbols can be viewed as functions with arity zero. In addition there is a set of logical symbols (independent of $\mathcal{L}$) including the connectives $\wedge, \vee, \neg$, the equality predicate $=$, and the constant predicates **true** and **false**. A countably infinite set of variables $x_1, x_2, \ldots$ is also available.

Two classes of syntactical expressions can be formed over the symbols of $\mathcal{L}$: terms and formulas. Terms are constants, variables, or functions with terms as arguments: e.g., c_1, x_4, $f_1(x_4, f_2(c_1))$. Formulas are (*i*) *atoms* — that is, predicates with terms as arguments: e.g., true, $p_1(f_1(x_2))$, $f_1(x_1) = c_1$; (*ii*) connectives with formulas as arguments: e.g., $\neg p_1(x_1) \vee p_2()$; or (*iii*) quantified formulas, of the form $\forall x_i \mathcal{F}$ or $\exists x_i \mathcal{F}$, where $\mathcal{F}$ is a formula.

A *sentence* is a formula with no free variables. A *literal* is an atom or the negation ($\neg$) of an atom. A *clause* is a formula of the form $\ell_1 \vee \ldots \vee \ell_n$, where each ℓ_i is a literal. Clauses may also be quantified. It is often useful to represent the clause with no literals, using the symbol $\square$. Clause C_1 is a *variant* of clause C_2 if it differs only in the naming of variables and in the ordering and replication of literals. Thus $p(f(x)) \vee q(y)$ is a variant of $p(f(z)) \vee q(x) \vee p(f(z))$. A clause is *Horn* if at most one literal is positive.

A formula $\mathcal{F}$ is said to be in *prenex conjunctive normal form* (CNF) if it is in the form $Q_1 C_1 \wedge \ldots \wedge Q_n C_n$, where Q_i are (possibly empty) quantifications, and C_i are clauses. A sentence is said to be in *clause form* if it is in prenex CNF, with only universal ($\forall$) quantifications. If such a sentence contains only Horn clauses, it is called a Horn sentence. The (empty) sentence with no clauses is sometimes needed, and is written $\emptyset$.

The *Herbrand universe* H of terms over $\mathcal{L}$ is the set of all variable-free atoms. An (Herbrand) *interpretation* (or *model*) M is a set of atoms of the form $p_i(t_1, \ldots, t_n)$ where each $t_i \in H$, for $1 \leq i \leq n$. *Ground* is synonymous with *variable-free*. If α is a ground atom, then the Herbrand model M *verifies* (or *satisfies*) α if $\alpha \in M$; this is denoted $M \models \alpha$. If M does not verify α, then it satisfies $\neg \alpha$. The definition of verification can also be extended to formulas in general. A formula is called a *tautology* if it is satisfied by every model. The sentences true and $\emptyset$ are tautologies. If it is satisfied by no model, it is said to be *unsatisfiable*. false and $\square$ are unsatisfiable.

The connective $\rightarrow$ is defined in terms of $\wedge$ and $\neg$: $\mathcal{F}_1 \rightarrow \mathcal{F}_2$ means $\neg\mathcal{F}_1 \vee \mathcal{F}_2$. There are many ways to define logical proof systems on formulas. If the formulas are in clause form, resolution is one such system. If a sentence $\mathcal{F}$ is provable from only axiomatic assumptions, we write $\vdash \mathcal{F}$. If $\mathcal{F}_1$ is provable assuming that $\mathcal{F}_2$ is valid, we write $\mathcal{F}_2 \vdash \mathcal{F}_1$. In standard first-order logic, $\vdash \mathcal{F}_2 \rightarrow \mathcal{F}_1$ iff $\mathcal{F}_2 \vdash \mathcal{F}_1$.

3.6.2 Proof of Theorem 3.32

The proof has two parts: to show that, if $\varphi_2 \in \hat{\rho}(\varphi_1)$, then $\varphi_1 \succeq \varphi_2$; and to show that, if $h(\varphi_2) \subseteq h(\varphi_1)$, then φ_2 (or some equivalent) is in $\hat{\rho}^*(\varphi_1)$.

The first part is easy: if $\varphi_2 \in \hat{\rho}(\varphi_1)$, then φ_1 logically implies φ_2. This is a matter of checking that each rule in $\hat{\rho}$ preserves implications. For example, if we obtain φ_2 by deleting a clause in φ_1, then clearly, $\varphi_1 \vdash \varphi_2$.

For the second part, assume that $h(\varphi_2) \subseteq h(\varphi_1)$, so that $\varphi_1 \rightarrow \varphi_2$ is provable. We claim that φ_2 (or some equivalent[3]) belongs to $\hat{\rho}^*(\varphi_1)$. Assume that $\varphi_2 = \kappa_1 \wedge \cdots \wedge \kappa_r$ and that φ_2 is a logical consequence of φ_1. There is a resolution proof $\varphi_1 \vdash \varphi_2$, and hence $\varphi_1 \vdash \kappa_i$ for each $1 \leq i \leq r$. Our approach is to use the resolution proof of κ_i from φ_1 to construct a $\hat{\rho}$-refinement path from φ_1 to $\varphi_1 \wedge \kappa_i$. We can repeat this construction for each i and thereby show inductively that

---

[3]Henceforth we shall not distinguish variants of clauses and sentences, but instead treat them as identical.

$\varphi_1 \wedge \varphi_2 \in \hat{\rho}^*(\varphi_1)$. By deleting in succession the clauses of φ_1 (via rule $\hat{\rho}(1)$) we can continue the refinement from $\varphi_1 \wedge \varphi_2$ to φ_2, demonstrating that $\varphi_2 \in \hat{\rho}^*(\varphi_1)$. So the proof reduces to the case that φ_2 is a clause κ.

For the special case where κ is a tautology, we repeatedly apply the rule $\hat{\rho}(1)$ to derive the empty sentence, which is is equivalent to κ. Let us therefore assume that κ is not a tautology.

In the special case where φ_1 is unsatisfiable, it is easy to obtain $\varphi_1 \wedge \kappa$ for any clause κ: we can derive $\varphi_1 \wedge \square$ by resolution steps, use ρ_c to refine $\square$ into κ, and finally use $\hat{\rho}(1)$ to remove the clauses of φ_1. Let us therefore assume that φ_1 is satisfiable.

We may also assume that every clause in φ_1 and κ has its its own set of variables, disjoint from those found in all other clauses. There is a resolution proof $\varphi_1 \vdash \kappa$, consisting of a derivation of the empty clause $\square$ from the clauses of φ_1 and $\neg\kappa$. Let $\kappa = \forall \bar{e}(\beta_1(\bar{e}), \ldots, \beta_p(\bar{e}) \rightarrow \alpha_1(\bar{e}), \ldots, \alpha_n(\bar{e}))$ where $\bar{e}$ denotes the entire set of variables bound in κ. Then

$$\neg\kappa = \neg\forall\bar{e}\,(\alpha_1(\bar{e}) \vee \cdots \vee \alpha_p(\bar{e}) \vee \neg\beta_1(\bar{e}) \vee \cdots \vee \neg\beta_n(\bar{e}))$$
$$= \exists\bar{e}\,(\neg\alpha_1(\bar{e}) \wedge \cdots \wedge \neg\alpha_p(\bar{e}) \wedge \beta_1(\bar{e}) \wedge \cdots \wedge \beta_n(\bar{e}))$$

This sentence is not in clause form. To eliminate the $\exists$-quantifiers, we extend the language $\mathcal{L}$, for purposes of this proof, by introducing new "Skolem constants" $\bar{s}$, one for each variable in $\bar{e}$. Thus

$$\neg\kappa[\bar{s}] = \neg\alpha_1(\bar{s}) \wedge \cdots \wedge \neg\alpha_p(\bar{s}) \wedge \beta_1(\bar{s}) \wedge \cdots \wedge \beta_n(\bar{s}).$$

Each literal of $\neg\kappa[\bar{s}]$ is variable-free and acts as an independent clause in the resolution derivation of $\square$ from $\varphi_1 \wedge \neg\kappa[s]$. Note that there is a bijection $\theta_{\bar{s}}$ between the variables $\bar{e}$ occurring in $\kappa[\bar{e}]$ and the corresponding constants $\bar{s} \in \neg\kappa[\bar{s}]$. We shall utilize this correspondence later to restore uniquely the variables $\bar{e}$ to a formula with constants $\bar{s}$.

For an example of the steps described in this proof, refer to Example 3.34 below.

Since we shall be constructing a refinement path from φ_1 to κ based on the resolution proof, it is useful to assume that it has the following tabular format:

- Each step of the proof is numbered sequentially starting from 1, and contains a clause that either is one of the clauses from $\varphi_1 \wedge \neg\kappa$ (the "source" clauses), or is derived from two of the clauses in preceding steps ("predecessor clauses") by application of the resolution rule. The final step of the proof contains the empty clause, $\square$.

- For those steps whose clauses are formed by resolution, the atoms in each predecessor clause which were unified and eliminated by the resolution step are available in the table.

- For each line of the proof, as part of the construction we will add an additional clause (the "refinement" clause), as described below.

The proof proceeds by converting the resolution proof into a sequence of refinement steps. First, we give an algorithm to compute the refinement clause for each line. Then we prove some properties of these clauses that imply that they also correspond to $\hat{\rho}$-refinement steps. In particular, the refinement clause for the final line of the proof will be shown to be subclause of κ, and can be further refined to exactly κ by a sequence of ρ_c-refinements.

Algorithm for constructing refinement clauses:

The algorithm proceeds in two phases. First, clauses are computed for each line in terms of the constants $\bar{s}$. Then all occurrences of the Skolem constants are changed to their original variables in κ, using the substitution $\theta_{\bar{s}}$ described above.

Phase 1: For each line of the proof in sequence, beginning with the first, one of the following cases applies.

CASE 1: The clause C in the proof is a source clause. Then the refinement clause is the same as C.

CASE 2: Exactly one predecessor C_1 of the clause C in the proof comes from $\neg\kappa[\bar{s}]$ and the other C_2 does not. Let σ be the substitution used in resolving C_1 and C_2. Then if R_2 is the refinement clause corresponding to C_2, the refinement clause of C is $\sigma(R_2)$ – i.e., , the same substitution is applied to the refinement clause of the predecessor C_2.

CASE 3: Neither predecessor of the clause C in the proof comes from $\neg\kappa[\bar{s}]$. Then the refinement clause for C is obtained from those of the predecessors by applying the resolution rule, using the same substitution and atoms as used in the proof. This is always possible because (as we prove below) every refinement clause contains its corresponding proof clause as a sub-clause.

CASE 4: Both predecessors of the clause C in the proof come from $\neg\kappa[\bar{s}]$. But since both predecessors are atomic, C must be $\square$. This means that κ is a tautology. But we have assumed κ is not tautological; therefore *this case will not arise*.

Phase 2: For each line of the proof in sequence, beginning with the first, apply the substitution $\theta_{\bar{s}}$ to the refinement clause, replacing the constants $\bar{s}$ by the variables in κ from which they were obtained. $\diamond$

We now make the following three claims:

CLAIM 1: Every literal occurring in the refinement clause also occurs in in the corresponding proof clause.

CLAIM 2: The refinement clause for the last line is a non-empty subclause of κ.

CLAIM 3: Each rule in Phase I for deriving the refinement clause $R(\bar{s})$ from those of its predecessors corresponds to a $\hat{\rho}$-refinement operation that results in conjoining the clause $\theta_{\bar{s}}(R(\bar{s})$ to the original clause.

Given these results, we complete the proof as follows. Starting with the sentence φ_1, we can (using the third claim) add to the sentence each refinement clause occurring on the internal lines, using $\hat{\rho}$-refinement operations; we do so by adding first the refinement clauses for lines whose immediate predecessors are source clauses, then their successors, and so on, until the refinement clause R for the last line has been added. By the second claim, this clause is a non-empty subset of the literals of κ. The remaining literals of κ can be obtained by applying rule $\hat{\rho}(3)$, by Lemma 3.29. Finally, any extraneous clauses not in $\varphi_1 \wedge \kappa$ can be removed using rule $\hat{\rho}(1)$.

Proof of Claim 1: by induction on the resolution depth of the line. For source lines, this is immediate, since the proof and refinement clauses are identical, by Case 1.

Suppose that the refinement clause $R(\bar{s})$ is computed via the second case, with predecessor C_1 a ground literal from $\neg\kappa[\bar{s}]$ and the other C_2 inductively satisfying the claim. The resolution proof step that results in the clause C consists in unifying at least one literal in each of C_1 and C_2 via a substitution σ, then combining the clauses $\sigma(C_1)$ and $\sigma(C_2)$, and removing the unified literals. But C_1 is a single ground literal, so C is just $\sigma(C_2)$ with at least one literal removed. On the other hand, the resolution clause R is $\theta(R_2)$ (no literals are removed), hence $C \subseteq R(\bar{s})$.

Suppose that $R(\bar{s})$ is handled by Case 3, and the two predecessor lines satisfy the inductive hypothesis. The same literals removed from C_1 and C_2 by the resolution step are unified and removed from $R_1(\bar{s})$ and $R_2(\bar{s})$ and the same substitution is applied to the remaining literals. Hence the property is preserved. This concludes the proof of the first claim.

Proof of Claim 2: We observe first that only literals from κ will "survive" to reach the refinement clause R in the last step, since the other literals, originating from the clauses of φ_1, are resolved away by applications of Case 3. Literals from κ become part of the refinement clause when Case 2 is used: the substitution σ turns a literal in R_2 into a literal from κ. This literal will then be present in the refinement clauses of all lines derived from it, since no rules entail removing such literals. Thus if the final $R(\bar{s})$ were empty, then the result would be a proof of of $\square$ using only clauses from φ_1. But then φ_1 would be unsatisfiable, contrary to hypothesis. This proves the second claim.

Proof of Claim 3: Case 2 results in the substitution of a term for variables, since one of the two predecessors is a single literal from $\neg\kappa[\bar{s}]$. Clearly, the same result can be obtained using one or more applications of $\rho_c(2)$ (substituting a most-general term for variables).

Rule 3 is a resolution operation, which corresponds directly to $\hat{\rho}(2)$.

This completes the proof of the claim, and the theorem. □

Example 3.34 This example illustrates the preceding proof by showing how the clause κ can be derived by refinement from a sentence φ_1.

Let

$$\varphi_1 = \begin{cases} p_2(x_1) \to p_1(f_1(x_1)) \wedge \\ p_2(f_2(x_2)) \wedge \\ p_1(x_3), p_2(f_2(x_3)) \to p_3(f_3(x_3)) \end{cases}$$

$$\kappa[x] = p_2(f_1(x)), p_4(x,x) \to p_3(f_3(f_1(f_1(x))))$$

To construct the resolution proof $\varphi_1 \vdash \kappa$, we first find $\neg\kappa[x]$:

$$\neg\kappa[x] = \exists x (\neg p_3(f_3(f_1(f_1(x)))) \wedge p_2(f_1(x)) \wedge p_4(x,x)).$$

To convert this to clause form, introduce a constant value s for x (which exists, according to the $\exists x$). Then in the expanded language containing the new constant s,

$$\neg\kappa[s] = \begin{cases} \neg p_3(f_3(f_1(f_1(s)))) \wedge \\ p_2(f_1(s)) \wedge \\ p_4(s,s) \end{cases}$$

The bijection θ_s maps x to s.

The resolution proof is given in table form in Figure 3.4.   The

Each line of the resolution proof is given. Under "clauses", the first clause (C :) is the one used in the resolution proof; the indented clause (R :) is the "refinement" clause. Unifying substitutions are not shown.

LINE	CLAUSES	PREDECESSORS
1	$C : p_2(x_1) \rightarrow p_1(f_1(x_1))$	(φ_1)
	$R : p_2(x_1) \rightarrow p_1(f_1(x_1))$	
2	$C : p_2(f_2(x_2))$	(φ_1)
	$R : p_2(f_2(x_2))$	
3	$C : p_1(x_3), p_2(f_2(x_3)) \rightarrow p_3(f_3(x_3))$	(φ_1)
	$R : p_1(x_3), p_2(f_2(x_3)) \rightarrow p_3(f_3(x_3))$	
4	$C : p_3(f_3(f_1(f_1(s)))) \rightarrow \square$	$(\neg\kappa[s])$
	$R : p_3(f_3(f_1(f_1(x)))) \rightarrow \square$	
5	$C : p_2(f_1(s))$	$(\neg\kappa[s])$
	$R : p_2(f_1(x))$	
6	$C : p_4(s, s)$	$(\neg\kappa[s])$
	$R : p_4(x, x)$	

7	$C : p_1(f_1(f_1(s))), p_2(f_2(f_1(f_1(s)))) \rightarrow \square$	3, 4
	$R : p_1(f_1(f_1(x))), p_2(f_2(f_1(f_1(x)))) \rightarrow p_3(f_3(f_1(f_1(x))))$	
8	$C : p_2(f_2(f_1(f_1(s)))), p_2(f_1(s)) \rightarrow \square$	1, 7
	$R : p_2(f_1(x)), p_2(f_2(f_1(f_1(x)))) \rightarrow p_3(f_3(f_1(f_1(x))))$	
9	$C : p_2(f_1(s) \rightarrow \square$	2, 8
	$R : p_2(f_1(x)) \rightarrow p_3(f_3(f_1(f_1(x))))$	
10	$C : \square$	5, 9
	$R : p_2(f_1(x)) \rightarrow p_3(f_3(f_1(f_1(x))))$	

Figure 3.4: Resolution Proof Example.

first six lines are source clauses. Their refinement clauses are identical
(except for s and x) to their proof clauses, as called for by the first case
in the algorithm. Line 7 is obtained by resolving lines 3 and 4, with
the substitution $\sigma = \{x_3 \leftarrow f_1(f_1(s))\}$. Its proof clause is gotten by
application of the second case in the algorithm.

Line 8 is obtained by resolving lines 1 and 7, with the substitution
$\sigma = \{x_1 \leftarrow f_1(s)\}$. Its proof clause comes from applying the third case
in the algorithm. Line 9 is another instance of the third case.

Note that the refinement clause for line 10

$$R_{10} = p_2(f_1(x)) \rightarrow p_3(f_3(f_1(f_1(x))))$$

is a subclause of κ: only the literal $p_4(x,x)$ is omitted. To refine R_{10} to
κ, we use $\rho_c(3)$ to add the most-general literal $p_4(x_1,x_2)$, then $\rho_c(1)$ to
unify x_1 and x_2, and finally $\rho_c(1)$ to unify x_1 and x. $\triangle$

3.6.3   Refinement Properties of Figure 3.2

In Example 3.2 we claim without proof that the relation γ' defined in
Figure 3.2 is a correct, locally finite upward refinement. How does
one justify this claim, given that γ defined in Figure 3.1 is a correct
refinement?

We use the infix notation $\alpha \xrightarrow{\gamma} \beta$ and $\alpha \xrightarrow{\gamma'} \beta$ to denote single-step
derivations; $\alpha \xrightarrow{\gamma} * \beta$ and $\alpha \xrightarrow{\gamma'} * \beta$ indicate zero or more steps.

The correctness argument is easy. It begins by showing that if $e_1 \xrightarrow{\gamma'}$
e_2 then $e_1 \xrightarrow{\gamma} * e_2$ — i.e., any refinements of e_1 derivable with γ' are also
derivable by γ. In most cases the rules of γ_2 are instances of γ_1 rules,
so the proof is direct. For an inductive rule such as

if $e_1 \xrightarrow{\gamma'} e_1'$ then $e_1 \vee e_2 \xrightarrow{\gamma'} e_1' \vee e_2$

we argue thus: Suppose that $e_1 \xrightarrow{\gamma'} e_1'$, and that inductively $e_1 \xrightarrow{\gamma} e_1'$. Then $e_1 \vee e_1' \approx e_1'$ is derivable in $\xrightarrow{\gamma}$; and our task is to show that $(e_1 \vee e_2) \vee (e_1' \vee e_2) \approx e_1' \vee e_2$. Starting with the expression $(e_1 \vee e_2) \vee (e_1' \vee e_2)$, after a few easy steps this is $\approx (e_1 \vee e_1') \vee e_2$, and by substitution of e_1' for $e_1 \vee e_1'$ this is $\approx e_1' \vee e_2$.

More work is required to show that if $e_1 \xrightarrow{\gamma} e_2$ then $e_1 \xrightarrow{\gamma'} * e_2$ (the completeness condition for γ_2). The first step is to derive a lemma arguing that, from the expression **false**, we can generalize to any expression, and from there we can further generalize to **true**.

For all expressions α, **false** $\xrightarrow{\gamma'} * \alpha$ and $\alpha \xrightarrow{\gamma'} *$ **true**.

The argument is straightforward, an induction on the structure of α, using the rules **false** $\xrightarrow{\gamma'} x_i$ and $x_1 \xrightarrow{\gamma'}$ **true** as the basis.

Next we show for each rule of the form $\alpha \approx \beta$ in γ that $\alpha \xrightarrow{\gamma'} * \beta$ and $\beta \xrightarrow{\gamma'} * \alpha$. For example, the Bounds axiom:

$$e_1 \wedge \textbf{false} \xrightarrow{\gamma'} * \textbf{true} \wedge \textbf{false} \xrightarrow{\gamma'} \textbf{false}$$

$$\textbf{false} \xrightarrow{\gamma'} \textbf{false} \wedge \textbf{false} \xrightarrow{\gamma'} * \textbf{false} \wedge e_1.$$

The reflexive and transitive axioms in γ are subsumed by the $*$ in $\xrightarrow{\gamma'} *$. The symmetry axiom is a bit more subtle: it is not true in general that if $\alpha_1 \xrightarrow{\gamma'} * \alpha_2$ then $\alpha_2 \xrightarrow{\gamma'} * \alpha_1$ (since $\xrightarrow{\gamma'} *$ may include generalization steps as well as equivalence steps). Instead, by showing for each rule $\alpha \approx \beta$ in γ (other than the symmetry rule itself) that $\alpha \xrightarrow{\gamma'} * \beta$ and $\beta \xrightarrow{\gamma'} * \alpha$ (e.g., as shown above for the Bounds axiom), the symmetry axiom is obviated. Finally, for the generalization rule, we prove:

if $e_1 \vee e_2 \overset{\gamma'}{\to} * e_2$ then $e_1 \overset{\gamma'}{\to} * e_2$

as follows: $e_1 \overset{\gamma'}{\to} e_1 \vee (e_1 \wedge \textbf{false}) \overset{\gamma'}{\to} e_1 \vee \textbf{false} \overset{\gamma'}{\to} * e_1 \vee e_2 \overset{\gamma'}{\to} * e_2$.

We have thus shown that γ' is a refinement for $\succeq$, since any γ_1 derivation can be transformed into a γ_2 derivation.

The argument that γ' is locally finite consists in showing that, for any expression α, each γ'-refinement step yields a finite number of instances. The argument, by induction on the structure of α, begins with $\alpha = \textbf{true}$ and $\alpha = \textbf{false}$ and is straightforward for the most part. The only trickiness comes with expressions of the form $\neg e_1$, where inductively only finitely many expressions derive from e_1. The only two applicable rules in Figure 3.2 for expressions of this form are:

if $e_1 \overset{\approx}{\to} e_1'$ then $\neg e_1 \overset{\approx}{\to} \neg e_1'$

if $e_1' \overset{\gamma}{\to} e_1$ then $\neg e_1 \overset{\gamma}{\to} \neg e_1'$.

With the first rule, by the inductive hypothesis only finitely many expressions $\neg e_1'$ are derived from $\neg e_1$, but the inductive argument for the second rule is a bit trickier. Observe that for each rule $\alpha \overset{\gamma}{\to} \beta$ in Figure 3.2 the size of α (as measured by the number of connectives) is the same as that of β. Thus there can be only finitely many e_1' such that $e_1' \overset{\gamma}{\to} e_1$, and correspondingly only finitely many expressions $\neg e_1'$ derivable by $\overset{\gamma}{\to}$ from $\neg e_1$.

Part II

Probabilistic Identification from Random Examples

Chapter 4

Probabilistic Approximate Identification

In this chapter and the next, we shall adopt a different model of identification in order to focus on two of the weaknesses of the preceding theory: the lack of robustness, and the lack of a complexity measure.

Robustness. We would like to devise algorithms that can tolerate a certain level of inaccuracy in the examples. But since identification in the limit requires that the procedure succeed for arbitrary presentations, then for some domains systematic errors (even if they affect only a single example) can make correct identification impossible. This suggests that we adopt models in which the presentation is a stochastic process, instead of a deterministic one. And since the teacher is probabilistic, the identification criteria will be as well.

Complexity. If we wish to classify identification problems using the tools of complexity theory, one approach is to adapt the Blum theory of complexity measures [13] to identification functions. Another (which we adopt) is to consider the concrete complexity of algorithms that halt. If the model is reasonable, we should be able to ask whether a given class of rules can be identified in time T or storage S. Since complexity theory concerns the rate of growth of a complexity measure with the size of the problem, we must also specify what we mean by the size of the input.

One way to approach these goals is to replace the "indifferent teacher" – i.e., the arbitrary but complete presentation – by a friendlier, but still limited, teacher. As recent examples of this approach, we may cite the work of Marron and Ko [43] on the complexity of identifying pattern languages from well-chosen positive examples and queries of the form "Is p a correct pattern?", and an algorithm [3] for identifying minimal finite automata from both examples and queries that return a counterexample for an incorrect hypothesis. See also [4] for general results concerning the complexity associated with different types of queries. However, we shall not adopt this approach.

Both this chapter and the next will make extensive use of probability theory. Primary references for standard results in this area are [68] and [23].

4.1   Probabilistic Identification in the Limit

As an initial approach, let us replace the "indifferent" teacher of Part I by an even more indifferent teacher, one which has almost no control over the presentation. We assume that the teacher consists of one who randomly and independently selects examples (with replacement) from a population, and classifies them as positive or negative according to the target. The distribution function P of the population is arbitrary, and may (or may not) depend upon the target; the identification algorithm does *not* know the distribution function.

This model captures many learning situations encountered in practice: examples of a disease are studied as they occur randomly in a population; examples of makes of cars are learned as they appear on the road; and so on. In each case, the learner derives examples randomly from some distribution which he does not know and over which he has no control.

The notation $P[S]$, where S is a set of examples, denotes the probability that an example is drawn belonging to the set S. As in preceding chapters, we shall assume that $\mathcal{E}$ is countable (unless stated otherwise), and that the set of examples is a subset of $\mathcal{E}$. Thus if $P[S] = 0$, then no examples in the set S will ever be presented.

Definition 4.1 Let e_0 be (h-equivalent to) the target rule, and e an arbitrary rule. Let S be the set of examples that agree with either e_0 or e, but not both. Then the *error* of e is defined to be $P[S]$, the probability that an example belongs to S.

The notation $e_1 \triangle e_2$ will be used henceforth to denote the set of examples that agree with one or the other of the expressions e_1 and e_2, but not both. Such an example suffices to distinguish the two rules from one another; and if one of them is the target, and the other a hypothesis, then the probability of such an example is the probability of a counterexample to the hypothesis.

Intuitively, we can envision a procedure that makes a guess after each example. With more examples, the hypotheses get progressively better at predicting the example. But we demand more than just gradual improvement: for stochastic convergence, the guesses must almost surely converge (in finite time) to one which has probability 0 of being contradicted by an example. Note, however, that the convergent hypothesis need not be correct; it can be wrong on sets of examples with zero probability of being presented. For example, in learning to identify makes of cars by observing them on the highway, we need not come up with a rule that correctly classifies Dusenbergs in an area where these never appear on the road.

Specifically, an algorithm is said to *identify the class $\mathcal{E}$ stochastically in the limit* if the following condition holds: for any $d_0 \in \mathcal{D}$, the algorithm guesses some hypothesis e all but finitely many times, and with probability one, the error of e is zero.

The following algorithm for stochastic identification in the limit corresponds to Algorithm 1.9.

Algorithm 4.2 (Stochastic Infinite Identification)
INPUT:

- A r.e. set $\mathcal{E} = e_1, e_2, \ldots$ of rules.
- An oracle EX for (random) examples.

- An oracle *GE?* for testing whether $h(e_i) \geq$ an example x.

OUTPUT:

A sequence H_1, H_2, ... of rules in $\mathcal{E}$.

PROCEDURE:

1. $i \leftarrow 1$.

2. Do forever:

    2.1 Get the next example $x = EX()$.

    2.2 While e_i disagrees with x, $i \leftarrow i + 1$.

    2.3 Output e_i.   ◇

Significantly, when comparing this algorithm to Algorithm 1.9, we note that no examples are stored. An algorithm with this property is often called *incremental*. Evidently, the probabilistic teacher is a much stronger source of information than the arbitrary complete presentation. Also, the algorithm suggests that we conduct a sequential search through the rules for one that agrees with the current example; but clearly a smarter search algorithm could be substituted (see Section 4.3).

In the correctness proof below, we shall require the following two popular lemmas.

Lemma 4.3 For all ϵ and all $n \geq 0$,

$$(1 - \epsilon)^n \leq e^{-\epsilon n},$$

with equality holding if and only if $\epsilon n = 0$.

PROOF: $e^{-\epsilon} = \sum_{i \geq 0}(-\epsilon)^i/i! \geq 1 - \epsilon$ (dropping all but two terms of the series). Now raise both sides to the power n.   □

Lemma 4.4 (Borel-Cantelli) Let $A_1, A_2, \ldots$ be an infinite sequence of events. If $\sum_n \Pr[A_n] < \infty$, then the probability that infinitely many A_n occur is 0.   □

Theorem 4.5 Algorithm 4.2 identifies $\mathcal{E}$ stochastically in the limit.

PROOF: Note that the algorithm can never discard a hypothesis with zero error; hence it suffices to show that every hypothesis preceding the first correct one in the enumeration of $\mathcal{E}$ will be discarded with probability one. Suppose a rule e with error $\epsilon > 0$ is the current hypothesis of the algorithm. For $n > 0$, let A_n be the event that e agrees with the first n examples presented after it becomes the current hypothesis. The probability of A_n is $(1 - \epsilon)^n \leq e^{-\epsilon n}$. But $\sum_{n \geq 1} e^{-\epsilon n} < \infty$. Thus, by the Borel-Cantelli lemma, a counterexample to e is eventually drawn with probability one, and e will be discarded.

□

A number of studies have considered the problem of probabilistic identification from positive examples only. To avoid overgeneralization, these procedures operate on domains for which a probability that e generates x can be computed for each rule e and example x. For example, Horning [32] devised a procedure for identifying stochastic context-free grammars; the probability associated with each production in the grammar assigns a probability to every word generated by the grammar. Rudich [59] studies the problem of identifying the structure (states and transitions) of a Markov chain from an infinite sequence of state transitions. The general problem of probabilistic identification from positive examples, however, remains an interesting open problem.

4.2 The Model of Valiant

The following model, suggested by Valiant [71], replaces the infinite process of probabilistic exact identification in the limit with a finite process, which we call *probabilistic, approximately correct identification* (or *pac-identification*).

4.2.1 *Pac*-Identification

As above, we assume that there is a distribution P from which the teacher EX independently draws examples and classifies them as positive or negative. The task of the identification procedure, however, is different. The procedure makes only one guess. Before doing so, it requests a finite number of examples from the teacher, which it uses to choose its answer.

Instead of requiring that the procedure output a guess with zero error, we require only that the error of the guess be as small as we choose, with high probability. The smaller the error we can tolerate, the more examples we must request.

Specifically, two positive fractions, ϵ and δ, are given to the procedure. The tolerance ϵ represents the maximum error allowed in the answer. δ specifies the maximum probability (over possible runs of the algorithm) that a hypothesis with error more than ϵ will result; $1 - \delta$

represents the confidence that a suitable hypothesis will result. Formally, the learning algorithm is to output a hypothesis e such that, if e_0 is a correct hypothesis,

$$\Pr\left[\mathcal{P}[e \triangle e_0] > \epsilon\right] < \delta. \tag{4.1}$$

For example, suppose the learner is trying to infer a rule characterizing catalpa trees from examples. The teacher, an expert in recognizing this type of tree, leads the learner through the local woods, where he identifies each tree as either belonging or not belonging to the catalpa sort. Not having had any control over the planting of the forest, the teacher cannot select his examples, but must be content with the existing distribution of such trees. The learner is prearmed with a set of possible criteria for forming his classification (leaf types, bark patterns, etc.), and wants to achieve 99% confidence that he will correctly recognize a randomly selected tree in that forest as being a catalpa or not. If there are very few catalpa trees in the forest, the learner's rule may be rather incomplete by botanical standards; but his success in learning is being judged only according to its success in that forest, not by some textbook criterion. It is also possible that the particular part of the forest selected by the teacher has a particularly skewed sample of catalpas, so the learner cannot rule out a small chance – say, 5% – that his classification rule will not achieve the 99% confidence rate over the forest as a whole[1].

---

[1] While illustrative, this example is not really accurate, since the teacher presumably is not selecting trees independently and randomly from the entire population of trees in the forest, but is drawing from a particular part of the forest where neighboring trees may be affected by conditions not present elsewhere in the forest.

It is important to emphasize, as in the previous section, that the learner need not know the distribution P. The requirement that the procedure work for an arbitrary P is stringent; but the error is measured with respect to the same distribution P, so that the algorithm cannot be faulted if it fails to account for features that occur only rarely.

To measure the complexity of the algorithm for a particular domain $\mathcal{E}$, we need to include the confidence and tolerance values; for as these approach zero, the required number of examples will increase. With respect to this model, a class $\mathcal{E}$ is said to be *pac-identifiable* if there is an algorithm with the following property: for any rule e_0 in $\mathcal{E}$, any distribution P of examples, and any positive fractional values of ϵ and δ, the algorithm pac-identifies e_0 after requesting m examples, where m depends upon ϵ and δ (but not P). The class is *polynomial-time (pac-)identifiable* if it is pac-identifiable, $m(\epsilon, \delta)$ is polynomial in $1/\epsilon$ and $1/\delta$, and the algorithm runs in time polynomial in the total size of the examples.

We may also consider how the time complexity increases with the size of the class $\mathcal{E}$. Suppose $\{\mathcal{E}_n\}_{n>1}$ is a family of domains parameterized by n, such that $\mathcal{E}_n \subseteq \mathcal{E}_{n+1}$ for $n \geq 1$. For example, if $\mathcal{E}_n$ is the class of all Boolean truth tables over n variables, the size of $\mathcal{E}_n$ grows at least doubly exponentially with n. A family of domains is said to be a *polynomial-time (pac-)identifiable* family if there is an pac-identification algorithm requesting $m(\epsilon, \delta, n)$ examples, where m is polynomial in n, $1/\epsilon$, and $1/\delta$, that runs in time polynomial in the size of the examples.

Example 4.6 (from [16]) Let $\mathcal{E}$ be a finite set of N rules, with the property that for any example x and for any rule $e \in \mathcal{E}$, there is an algorithm testing whether $h(e) \geq h(x)$ in time polynomial in the size of x. Then $\mathcal{E}$ is polynomial-time identifiable, as follows.

The procedure is to request $m = (1/\epsilon)\ln(N/\delta)$ examples and then output any rule which agrees with all these examples. Since some rule in $\mathcal{E}$ is correct, this is always possible. We can show that such a rule has error greater than ϵ only with probability less than δ. For, consider a rule e with error greater than ϵ. This means that the likelihood a random example agrees with e is less than $(1 - \epsilon)$; hence for m such examples, the likelihood that e agrees with all of them is less than $(1 - \epsilon)^m$, By Lemma 4.3, $(1 - \epsilon)^m \leq e^{-\epsilon m}$, and for the value of m above, this is bounded by δ/N. Finally, there are at most $N - 1$ such rules with unacceptably large error, and so the probability that any one of them agrees with all m examples is less than δ. The requirements for pac-identification are thus satisfied. $\triangle$

This example depends on the fact that the size of the class $\mathcal{E}$ is finite. The following algorithm pac-identifies any class (finite or otherwise), and represents a bridge between stochastic identification (an infinite process that almost surely yields a hypothesis with zero error) and pac-identification (a finite process that yields with high probability a hypothesis with small error).

The algorithm proceeds down the list of rules. For each rule in turn, it draws a certain number of examples, and if the rule agrees with all the examples, the algorithm halts and outputs the rule. Otherwise it tries the next rule.

Algorithm 4.7 *Pac*-Identification in the limit.

INPUT:

- A r.e. set $\mathcal{E} = e_1, e_2, \ldots$ of rules.
- Positive fractions ϵ and δ.
- A (probabilistic) oracle *EX* for examples.
- An oracle *GE?* for testing whether $h(e_i) \geq$ an example x.

OUTPUT:

A single rule $H \in \mathcal{E}$.

PROCEDURE:

1. $i \leftarrow 1$.

2. Repeat:

   2.1 Request $m(i)$ examples, where

   $$m(i) = \left\lceil \frac{1}{\epsilon} \left(i + \ln(1/\delta) \right) \right\rceil.$$

   2.2 If e_i disagrees with any of these examples, $i \leftarrow i + 1$.

   2.3 Else output e_i and halt.

   until it halts.   ◇

Theorem 4.8 Algorithm 4.7 *pac*-identifies $\mathcal{E}$.

PROOF: The algorithm halts, since there is a correct rule e_0 in $\mathcal{E}$ for which the halting condition will be satisfied. We need only be sure that it does not halt prematurely with a rule whose error is more than ϵ.

Consider the i'th round. If e_i has error more than ϵ, the likelihood that it will agree with all $m(i)$ examples is less than

$$(1 - \epsilon)^{m(i)} \leq e^{-\epsilon m(i)}$$
$$\leq \delta/e^i.$$

Suppose the first rule in $\mathcal{E}$ whose error is zero occurs in position r in the enumeration. Then the probability that the algorithm erroneously halts before getting to the r'th step is less than

$$\sum_{i=1}^{r-1} \frac{\delta}{e^i} < \delta.$$

$\square$

We may also note that it is not necessary for the algorithm to request $m(i)$ examples in the i'th round: if examples are retained, only enough additional examples are needed in each round to bring the total up to $m(i)$. This means that only $1/\epsilon$ new examples are needed in each round, after the first.

4.2.2   Identifying Normal-Form Expressions

For a finite domain $\mathcal{E}$ with N rules, pac-identification is data-efficient in that the number of examples required is proportional to $1/\epsilon$, $\log 1/\delta$, and most notably, $\log N$. Thus the number of rules in a family $\mathcal{E}_n$ of domains can grow exponentially in the parameter n, while the number of examples grows only polynomially. The time to execute the identification procedure, however, also depends upon the time to search for a rule in $\mathcal{E}_n$ that agrees with the examples. If the number of rules is exponential in n, can such a search be completed in time polynomial in n?

The answer to this question clearly depends on the domain. And an active area of research is concerned with determining the complexity of identifying various domains, especially propositional logic (e.g., [28], [36], [50]). For example we would like to be able to identify any rule from examples when the rule is expressed in DNF, as such rules are easy for humans to understand. Since unrestricted DNF formulas with n variables can express any of the 2^{2^n} Boolean functions on n variables, a superexponential number of examples will be required for pac-identification of this class [15]. Of course, most of these functions require a DNF formula of length exponential in n, but even if we permit the learner time polynomial in the length of the formula, this class is probably hard to identify [36]. So we focus instead on less expressive classes.

Valiant [71] showed that the class $CNF_n(k)$ of propositional formulas over n Boolean variables, in conjunctive normal form (CNF) with at most k literals in any clause, is polynomial-time identifiable (for fixed k) when the examples consist of satisfying truth assignments (i.e., only positive examples are given). Note that the number of possible clauses is at most $(2n + 1)^k$: for each of k "slots" in the clause, we may select as a literal any variable, its complement, or no variable at all. Since k is fixed, this is a polynomial in n. However, the number of possible *formulas* in $\mathcal{E}$ is exponentially higher, since a formula consists of a subset of the clauses. Hence it is an interesting result that, from among an exponentially large set of hypotheses, we can select an acceptable one in polynomial time. Let us show that Valiant's $CNF_n(k)$ result extends to the more general case of normal-form expressions over a monotonic operation (see Definition 3.13).

Assume that $\mathcal{E}$ has a downward-monotonic operation $\odot$ and enjoys a normal-form property with respect to this operation. (The dual result holds for an upward-monotonic operation from negative examples.) We shall require that the number of components be bounded; let M represent this number. Also, let the empty expression $\emptyset$, with no components, represent the upper-bounding expression: $h(\emptyset) \geq h(e)$ for all $e \in \mathcal{E}$.

The following simple observation is key: if c is a component that disagrees with the example x, then for any expression e, $c \odot e$ also disagrees with x. For, suppose $h(c \odot e) \geq h(x)$; then the monotonicity of $\odot$ implies that $h(c) \geq h(c \odot e) \geq h(x)$, contradicting the assumption that c disagrees with x. Thus the main idea of the identification algorithm is that we should eliminate components that disagree with the positive examples and retain those that agree.

We now assume that an oracle EX selects a target expression e_0 in $\mathcal{E}$ and a distribution P for the positive examples of e_0. Parameters ϵ and δ are given as input to the following identification procedure:

Algorithm 4.9 Identification of $\odot$-normal form formulas.
INPUT:

- A set of M components $c_1, \ldots, c_M$.

- An oracle EX for random examples.

- An oracle for testing a component against an example.

OUTPUT:

An $\odot$-normal form rule.

PROCEDURE:

1. Call $EX()$ for $m = (M/\epsilon)\ln(M/\delta)$ positive examples.
2. Test each component c_i $(1 \leq i \leq M)$ against the examples and mark those which agree with all m.
3. Output the normal-form expression consisting of all marked components joined by $\odot$. $\quad\diamond$

Theorem 4.10 Algorithm 4.9 *pac*-identifies the class of $\odot$-normal-form expressions in $\mathcal{E}$.

PROOF: Let us call a component *harmful* if the probability is at least ϵ/M that an example disagrees with it. Then for any normal-form expression that includes *all correct* components (Def. 3.17) and *no harmful* ones, the probability is at most ϵ that it will disagree with a random example (since there are at most M incorrect, non-harmful components).

We claim that the algorithm removes, with high probability, all harmful components and no correct ones. Since a correct component never disagrees with any example, it is clear that every correct component will be included. Suppose, however, that c is harmful, but nevertheless agrees with all m of the examples. The probability of this event is at most $(1 - \frac{\epsilon}{M})^m < e^{-\epsilon m/M}$. So the probability that *some* harmful component is not eliminated by a counterexample is less than $Me^{-\epsilon m/M}$. Substituting $m = \frac{M}{\epsilon}\ln\frac{M}{\delta}$ shows that this probability is less than δ. $\quad\square$

Using a more complicated argument, Valiant has shown that a sample size of $O((M+\ln(1/\delta))/\epsilon)$ is sufficient. Still, the number of examples depends on M, and for the case of $CNF_n(k)$, M is $O(n^k)$. If there are thousands of attributes, but a rule depends on only a few of them, we would like to be able to identify the rule with a much smaller set of examples. Hence, while Valiant has shown that there are exponential-size classes that can be identified in polynomial time, the algorithm cannot yet be considered practical.

Some further observations: (1) If $\mathcal{E}_n$ is a family of domains and M, the number of components, is super-polynomial in n, then this algorithm is not a polynomial-time identification procedure for the family. (2) The same algorithm pac-identifies $\mathcal{E}$ when the sample includes both positive and negative examples (simply by ignoring the negative examples).

4.2.3 Related Results about Valiant's Model

Others have contributed results about this model. Pitt and Valiant [50] obtained a number of negative results, showing that certain classes of formulas are not polynomial-time learnable unless $NP = R$ [2]; these classes include DNF_n formulas over n variables, even if the formulas are restricted to at most two monomial terms, and the class of Boolean threshold formulas. Angluin [3] showed that the class of n-state minimal finite acceptors for regular sets is polynomial-time learnable with the help of an oracle able to answer questions of the form, "Is the string w in the target set?".

Blumer *et al.* [15] consider the special case of concept learning, in

---

[2]R is the class of sets recognizable in random polynomial time.

which the rules $\mathcal{E}$ represent subsets of a universe U and examples are (expressions representing) elements of U. They consider the case where $\mathcal{E}$ and U may be uncountable, as in the case of some classes of geometric concepts in Euclidean space R^n. Their primary contribution is the significance of the *Vapnik-Chervonenkis dimension* to polynomial-time learnability.

The Vapnik-Chervonenkis dimension (or simply, the dimension) is a measure of the expressiveness of the class $\mathcal{E}$. Let S be a subset of U. Each rule e can be thought of as splitting S into two parts: those elements that are positive examples of e and those that are *negative* examples of e. There are $2^{|S|}$ ways to split S; if for each of these there is a corresponding hypothesis in $\mathcal{E}$, then $\mathcal{E}$ is said to *shatter* S. A remarkable fact is that either $\mathcal{E}$ shatters every subset of U, or there is an integer d such that no subset of U with more than d elements is shattered by $\mathcal{E}$. If such a d exists for $\mathcal{E}$, then $\mathcal{E}$ is called a *Vapnik-Chervonenkis class* (V-C class) of dimension d. If no such d exists, then the dimension of the class is said to be infinite.

Example 4.11 Let I be the class of open intervals on the real line $\mathcal{R}$. Then I is a V-C class of dimension 2: two points $\{x, y\}$ in $\mathcal{R}$ can be shattered by intervals covering both points, neither point, or any one of the points. But for any three points $x < y < z$, the subset $\{x, z\}$ cannot be represented in an open interval without including y. And this clearly holds for more than three points, also.

By contrast, the class of open *sets* over $\mathcal{R}$ has infinite dimension, since for any finite set of points we can cover any subset of them with open neighborhoods around the included points.

If $\mathcal{E}$ is a finite class $\{e_1, \ldots, e_n\}$, then the dimension is at most $\lfloor \log_2 n \rfloor$, since any set of p points requires 2^p different concepts to be shattered. $\triangle$

The main result of [15] is:

Theorem 4.12 A class $\mathcal{E}$ is pac-identifiable if and only if the dimension of $\mathcal{E}$ is finite.

$\square$

They show that, if d is the dimension of $\mathcal{E}$, then *any* algorithm which requests at least

$$m = \max \left[\frac{4}{\epsilon} \log_2 \frac{2}{\delta}, \frac{8d}{\epsilon} \log_2 \frac{8d}{\epsilon} \right] \qquad (4.2)$$

examples and finds a rule e consistent with these examples is an algorithm for pac-identifying $\mathcal{E}$. Note that m is polynomial in $1/\epsilon$ and $\log 1/\delta$, so that if there is a polynomial-time algorithm that finds a rule consistent with a set of examples, the class is polynomial-time identifiable.

Thus, referring to the preceding example, the class I of open intervals is polynomial-time pac-identifiable, since we can find a consistent hypothesis quickly by taking an open interval from the smallest to the largest positive sample point (excluding any negative example points). The class of open intervals is *not* pac-identifiable.

Note that it is possible to identify even an uncountable domain when its dimension is finite. So far we have considered only countable sets $\mathcal{E}$, but finite-dimension VC classes have a finite character which limits their expressiveness on finite sets of examples.

Haussler [28] suggests using the dimension to quantify the inductive bias in an algorithm, and shows that a class of propositional formulas with internal disjunctions and compound terms, similar to the APC formulas used by Michalski, have finite dimension and are polynomial-time identifiable. In that paper, he also considers a probabilistic approach to the Version Space model, noting that all rules with error $> \epsilon$ can be eliminated with probability at least $(1 - \delta)$, using at most $(1/\epsilon) \ln(|\mathcal{E}|/\delta)$ examples, where $|\mathcal{E}|$ is the number of rules in the space. This can mean a significant efficiency improvement over exhaustive search algorithms. (See also Section 4.3 below.)

The usefulness of the Vapnik-Chervonenkis dimension is limited by the fact that it currently applies only to concept-learning domains. As we have seen, it is often important to consider domains for which the set of examples is not necessarily limited to singleton sets. Generalizing this notion to arbitrary sets of examples would be quite interesting.

With the above and other results, interest in Valiant's model of identification has grown. One of its principal contributions to the theory is the ability to measure the computational complexity of identification problems. Unfortunately, the results suggest that many natural domains of interest are probably computationally intractable in this model (for example, DNF_n formulas as noted above). Does this mean that the model is too stringent in its requirements? Probably not. The complexity in these problems arises, not so much from the requirement that P be arbitrary or that sample sizes be polynomial in $1/\epsilon$, $1/\delta$, and n, but from the difficulty of searching for a formula that agrees with the examples. The negative complexity results may indicate that efficient learning requires the assistance of deductive reasoning or a previously induced bias for a more efficient representation.

4.3   Using the Partial Order

The most difficult part of the pac-identification task is generally the search for a rule consistent with the finite set of training examples. Can the underlying ordering of the rule space (which, after all, led to the Refinement Model of Part I) be used to speed up this search?

Recall that, by assumption, the semantic set D is partially ordered by $\geq$, and that $\mathcal{E}$ is ordered by $\succeq$. Let $\mathcal{E}$ be finite, and let σ be a finite set of examples (both positive and negative). Testing a rule e against σ, results in one of the following:

1. e agrees with all examples in σ. Then no revision in the hypothesis is required.

2. e agrees with all the positive examples, but covers at least one negative example. Then in searching for a rule e' that agrees with σ, we can eliminate e and any rule which is more general than e.

3. e excludes all negative examples, but also excludes at least one positive example. Then we can eliminate e and any rule which is more specific than e.

4. e disagrees with at least one positive and at least one negative example. Then we should consider only those rules that are incomparable to (neither more general nor more specific than) e.

Thus, testing a hypothesis e against a set σ of examples can be interpreted as giving information about the relationship of the target e_0

to e in the ordering. An interesting question is: can we determine, by preprocessing the ordering, in what sequence in which to test the rules so as to minimize the number of rules that must be tested?

The results of such a preprocessing algorithm can be represented by a decision tree, whose internal nodes specify that a rule be tested against the examples in σ. There are up to four descendents of such a node, corresponding to the four outcomes listed above:

1. the subtree is a leaf, specifying that the tested rule is consistent with σ and therefore a target of the search.

2. the subtree is a decision tree for the remaining elements after eliminating those above the tested rule in the ordering.

3. the subtree is a decision tree for the remaining elements after eliminating those below the tested rule in the ordering.

4. the subtree is a decision tree for the elements incomparable to the tested node.

The height of this decision tree is the number of rules that must be tested in the worst case.

Unfortunately, constructing optimal decision trees of this type seems to be a hard problem (*cf.* [41]). And even the optimal decision tree may not significantly reduce the number of tests.

The refinement techniques of Part I can also be used to direct the search: e.g., given an upward refinement γ, after testing the rule e against the examples, we would compute $\gamma(e)$ in case (3), but merely discard the rule in cases (2) and (4). Any other techniques for quickly finding a rule consistent with a finite set of examples can be applied. But such techniques depend on the properties of the domain.

4.4   Summary

We have considered the problem of identification from a teacher who presents examples at random, as distinguished from a teacher who fixes a deterministic presentation beforehand. For identification in the limit, the same simple strategy used for identification-by-enumeration algorithms works here: select a hypothesis consistent with the examples. A major advantage of the probabilistic model is that examples do not have to be stored. For *pac*-identification, consistency is with respect to a finite set of examples. We can compute the number of examples required for *pac*-convergence, and in general a feasible number suffices. Another advantage is that the algorithms are finite, and their complexities can be studied and compared.

On the other hand, the search for a consistent rule can be computationally difficult for some domains. Whether or not the underlying partial order for rules can be of use in speeding up the worst-case time for this search depends on both the particular ordering and the class of examples.

A thorny problem which plagues all of the algorithms so far is that of sensitivity to even very small amounts of noise in the examples. We need new ideas to solve this problem.

Chapter 5

Identification from Noisy Examples

5.1 Introduction

When some of the training examples may be incorrect, none of the foregoing identification strategies are effective:

- With algorithms based on identification by enumeration (including refinement algorithms), an incorrect example may cause a correct hypothesis to be discarded. Even if correct hypotheses occur infinitely often in the enumeration, errors can cause them to be discarded infinitely often, and thereby frustrate convergence.

- With pac-identification, the fundamental strategy of choosing a hypothesis consistent with the examples may fail, because there may be no such hypothesis.

135

Our goal is to replace these strategies by ones that are effective for classes of random errors in the training data. The emphasis will be on concepts applicable to many domains.

Noise. In this dissertation we limit consideration to the case of independent, random errors ("noise") in the training examples. Specifically, we assume there is a constant probability that any example will be affected in any way by errors, and that this probability is independent of whether any other examples have been so affected. The event of presenting an example to the identification algorithm can be modeled by a "noisy" oracle, EX_η, which we think of as the familiar reliable oracle $EX()$ followed by a random noise process NP_η. The latter, with constant probability η, changes a valid example $\langle s, x \rangle$ into $\langle s', x' \rangle$ before presenting it to the identification algorithm. The possible values of $\langle s', x' \rangle$ will depend on the specific type of noise processes; we shall consider several of these.

Correspondence Principle. We should also expect that a Correspondence Principle applies to the solution: that as the rate η of errors approaches zero, the algorithm should revert either to one of our algorithms for identification from reliable data or to a new one. Said somewhat differently, the solution should vary continuously with η as $\eta \to 0$. Strategies that are radically different when η is any positive value, however small, from when $\eta = 0$ are not "robust" and probably overlook some fundamental feature of the identification process.

Dependence on error rate. The algorithms we propose should not require as input the actual rate of error. Instead, the algorithm should either determine an estimate of the rate of error as part of the identification procedure, or require as input at most an upper bound on the rate of error.

A general strategy. We propose and analyze the following simple strategy: *of the candidate hypotheses, choose one which agrees with the highest proportion of the examples presented.* We shall demonstrate that, with a sufficiently large set of examples, this strategy can be used as the basis for both identification in the limit and pac-identification. In the Valiant model, we can calculate the number of training examples needed to within fairly close limits. We shall also find that the same analysis techniques apply to many different noise processes. And we should note that this strategy satisfies the Correspondence Principle: as $\eta \to 0$, "best agreement" approaches "exact agreement", the criterion for both identification by enumeration and pac-identification strategies.

Summary of results. Following a review of previous research pertaining to identification from unreliable data, we introduce the new ideas by initially restricting attention to a simple class of random errors, the *Classification Noise Process*. Algorithms are given both for identification in the limit and for pac-identification within this class of noise.

We then embark on a merry course of generalizing the results of Chapter 4 so as to encompass noise. The algorithm for normal-form identification brings to bear a negative result: finding a most-consistent hypothesis may be a hard problem computationally for some domains. Nevertheless, there is a polynomial-time generalization for the corresponding (noise-free) algorithm of Section 4.2.2. We then show how the preceding ideas can be modified for the case of noise processes other than the simple Classification Noise Process, and show how an identification procedure can often be coaxed into determining the noise rate η for itself.

5.2　Prior Research Results

Many people have regretfully observed that their identification algorithms depend rather strongly on the assumption of error-free data, and that this assumption is generally unrealistic. Few, however, have suggested any way to make their algorithms error tolerant, and fewer still have sought ways that satisfy the Correspondence Principle.

A number of heuristic approaches have been suggested, and while most have treated the case of random noise, Schlimmer and Granger [64] consider systematic errors and concept "drift". They study the effect of these on a concept-learning algorithm that has previously converged to a hypothesis (in the limiting sense). Systematic errors take the form of attribute values that are consistently reported incorrectly – e.g., a rain gauge always reads below, never above, the actual precipitation amount. Drift occurs when some of the attributes of the target concept change continuously over time – e.g., an animal's color changes with season or surroundings. Their system identifies concepts represented by Boolean formulas in DNF, with two weights for the terms – one for the sufficiency of the term and one for its necessity. Using Bayesian statistics, they report that their system can track concept drift and distinguish it from the introduction of systematic noise. However, it is difficult to see what properties of their system are due to statistical processes and how one might apply the ideas to more general situations. Also, the factors determining the number of examples required are not evident, so it is difficult to estimate the amount of data required.

Wilkins and Buchanan [75] also consider heuristic identification of Boolean expressions. Their system takes a large collection of MYCIN-type rules with associated confidence factors, and tries to edit the rules and factors so as to account for a noisy set of data. One basic strategy – to maximize agreement with the data – is found to be NP-Complete, but a heuristic approximation algorithm is proposed.

Quinlan [54] reports what is perhaps the most thorough experimental study of identification from noisy data, and draws some general conclusions from the results. He modified his ID3 program substantially in order to handle random errors in each attribute and also classification errors. Of two different strategies for choosing a hypothesis to explain the noisy data, he (like Wilkins and Buchanan) found that choosing the one which minimizes the frequency of disagreement with the data was superior. Generally speaking, classification noise (noise affecting only the sign of the examples) was found to be a more significant pertubation than attribute noise.

In [61] and [62], Schäfer studies identification in the limit from examples with discrepancies, using the recursion-theoretic approach. She defines an n-anomalous presentation of a function ϕ to be a sequence σ of (x, y)-pairs such that

- $x \in \mathrm{dom}(\phi)$ (the domain of definition of function ϕ);
- for all $x \in \mathrm{dom}(\phi)$, $(x, \phi(x)) \in \sigma$;
- for all but n values of x, if $(x, y_1) \in \sigma$ and $(x, y_2) \in \sigma$ then $y_1 = y_2 = \phi(x)$.

Thus σ enumerates the graph of ϕ except that there may be a finite number of domain values x for which additional values besides $\phi(x)$ are presented. She also defines a *-anomalous presentation for which any finite number of anomalies are possible in the presentation. The procedure is permitted to converge to any function ϕ' which agrees with ϕ on all points in its domain presented without anomalies, and for which σ is a presentation of ϕ'.

Following the approach of this type of study, she does not construct algorithms, but considers classes of identifiable sets and demonstrates the existence of hierarchies of identifiable classes based on the number of anomalies and other restrictions on the algorithms. In addition, she shows that relaxing the number of output "mistakes" tolerated in the identification procedure does not assist in overcoming input anomalies.

For probabilistic identification, fewer results are available. Vapnik [74], studying the statistical problem of choosing a rule which best accounts for empirical data, assumes a model of random noise in which the rate of error may depend upon the content of the example. That is, instead of a uniform error rate η for all examples drawn from the distribution P, there is a probability $\eta(x)$ for each example value x that the example will be classified as positive, and $1 - \eta(x)$ that it will be classified as negative. His procedure is not concerned with identification, but with finding the classification rule that is statistically most successful for an unknown population of data. It is interesting how similar his analysis is to that presented in Section 5.4 despite the different nature of his objectives. But with his noise model, the most consistent rule may have more than the allowable rate of error ϵ with unacceptably large probability, so that *pac*-identification may not be possible. (More on this later.)

Valiant [72], whose algorithm for identifying $CNF_n(k)$ expressions was discussed in the preceding chapter, considers how that algorithm (and its dual for $DNF_n(k)$) can be extended to handle a small rate of errors in the examples — errors possibly chosen in the most damaging way by an adversary. For each example, a biased coin is flipped, and if it comes up heads (with probability $(1 - \eta)$) an example is drawn and correctly classified as before. If, however, it comes up tails (with probability η), an adversary is allowed to choose and classify (perhaps incorrectly) the example.

Valiant's result shows that for a very low rate of error $\eta \ll \epsilon$, his algorithm can be modified to achieve *pac*-identification. He suggests that only low error rates in general can be permitted if successful identification is to be possible. And for adversarial errors, this is the case; but we shall demonstrate that for other types of data errors, a substantial rate of errors can be accommodated.[1]

Horning [32], whose work has been previously mentioned, found an interesting algorithm for identifying stochastic unambiguous context-free grammars in the limit from a stochastic presentation. The presentation consists of the strings in the target stochastic grammar, occurring (with probability one) in sequence at the same rate as their probability

---

[1]Very recent results [37] have established tight bounds on the feasible rate of adversarial errors, as well as extensions of results appearing in [6] and [7].

of being generated by the target grammar. As an afterthought, he considers the implications of random noise for the algorithm, and finds that, given some rather extensive information about the statistical properties of the noise, he can generalize his algorithm in a straightforward way to handle the noise. Significantly he notes that his extension satisfies (what we have called) the Correspondence Principle. He then goes on to show how to estimate the noise rate in the data, given an upper bound less than one, using as estimators the frequency (in an initial segment of the example data) of words having probability zero in the hypothesis grammar. A similar idea will be used in Section 5.4.3.

5.3 The Classification Noise Process

For most of the analysis we shall consider a simple class of noise, for which the analysis is especially clear. Later (Section 5.7) we shall argue that most of the analysis can be extended to apply to other classes of noise as well.

Classification noise occurs when an expression e is obtained according to the distribution P and classified correctly (+ or −) by the oracle EX; but before the example is presented to the identification procedure, a demon reverses the sign of the example. Thus the example $\langle +, x \rangle$ is converted to $\langle -, x \rangle$, or $\langle -, x \rangle$ to $\langle +, x \rangle$, with the result that the learner is given an incorrect example. Clearly, a demon with unlimited power to misclassify at will can obliterate the information in the data and make identification impossible. If, however, the demon is handed a biased coin and told that whenever the coin comes up "heads" he can misclassify the example, then enough information about the target may survive, provided the "heads" do not occur too frequently. More practically, errors in the data may resemble classification noise when the teacher makes occasional, unpredictable errors in classifying the examples.

The precise definition of the Classification Noise Process (CNP) is as follows:

> Independently for each example, after it has been selected and classified but before presentation to the identification algorithm, the sign of the example is reversed with probability η.

For example, we can envision a concept-learning system which is learning to classify objects according to certain attributes. Under the CNP model, some of the training examples ("That car is a Bentley") are wrong, in the sense that the classification is wrong (the car really is a Packard), but the attributes are observed correctly. An error rate $\eta = 10\%$ means that on average one example in ten is misclassified.

It is easy to see that for $\eta = 1/2$, all of the information in the examples is obliterated by the noise. The learner could then replace the teacher by a coin flip and then "teach himself"; and it is hard to see how *pac*-identification could be achieved for this much noise. For noise rates above one half, the most successful hypotheses before the advent of noise become proportionately the least successful with the noise. Consequently if the learner cannot know whether $\eta > \frac{1}{2}$ or $\eta < \frac{1}{2}$, the identification procedure is liable to infer the complement of a good rule rather than the rule itself.

Based on these observations, *we shall limit the rate of noise η to less than one half*. Later, the mathematics will support the intuition that this restriction is generally necessary.

Let us study now the effect of classification noise on the performance of the rules. Consider a rule e with error p — i.e., without the noise, the rule will *fail* (disagree with an example) on average pm times in m examples. With the addition of noise, it may fail more often or less; we can calculate its expected failure rate p_η as follows:

$$p_\eta = (1 - \eta)p + \eta(1 - p). \qquad (5.1)$$

The first term states that, if no classification error occurs (probability $(1 - \eta)$) the probability of failure is p. The second term states that, if a classification error does strike (probability η), the rule will fail only if it would not have failed without the error, with probability $(1 - p)$.

Two special cases are of interest:

- When $p = 0$ (i.e., , the hypothesis has zero error), its failure rate increases to η with noise.

- When $p \geq \epsilon$, its failure rate is at least $\eta + \epsilon(1 - 2\eta)$; and since $(1 - 2\eta) > 0$, this failure rate is greater than that of any correct hypothesis (or one with zero error).

We shall call rules with error greater than ϵ *ϵ-bad*. Rules that are not ϵ-bad will be described as *ϵ-good*. Rules with zero error are described simply as *good*. A *correct* rule is one that is h-equivalent to the target.

The simple analysis above shows that, on average, ϵ-bad rules have a failure rate that is greater than that of good rules by at least $\epsilon(1 - 2\eta)$. We shall take advantage of this statistical difference to discriminate between these two classes of rules.

The main statistical tool for this purpose is the Law of Large Numbers. In its most basic form, it says that for sufficiently many tests of an event whose probability of occurring is p, the fraction $\hat{p}$ of the tests on which the event occurs will be arbitrarily close to p, with high probability. More precisely, in m trials, as $m \to \infty$,

$$\Pr\left[|p - \hat{p}| > \epsilon\right] \to 0,$$

for all $\epsilon > 0$. Theorems are available to enable us to estimate how large m must be in order to reduce this probability below a given amount δ.

Relating this to the preceding discussion, we "test" a hypothesis by drawing examples; a failure on the example is an "event". If a correct hypothesis fails on average at the rate η, then with enough examples m we will measure a failure rate (number of disagreements divided by m) arbitrarily close to η, with high probability. Similarly, an ϵ-bad rule will fail at very nearly its expected rate, $\eta + s$, where $s \geq \epsilon(1 - 2\eta) > 0$. Thus we can force the probability to be as high as we want that good rules will fail less often on the examples than ϵ-bad rules. This is the basis for most of the algorithms in this section.

5.4 *Pac*-Identification

5.4.1 Finite Classes

In Example 4.6 we considered the problem of pac-identification for an arbitrary finite set of rules. Let us reconsider this procedure when classification errors are possible. The analysis is fairly straightforward, and yet many of the ideas extend to other, more complex, cases.

As an example scenario, suppose we are once again trying to learn to identify catalpa trees from a teacher by taking a random walk in the woods. We have a finite set of attributes (leaf type, bark texture, etc.), each with a finite number of possible values, with which to make the discrimination. Instead of a professional botanist, however, our teacher is a graduate assistant whose mind is on other matters much of the time. Occasionally, therefore, our teacher commits a classification error — either falsely asserting that a tree is a catalpa, or declaring that it is some other tree when it is in fact a catalpa. We have no way of knowing how often the teacher errs on average, but there is good reason to believe that this rate is substantially less than one half.

As before, we let $\mathcal{E} = \{e_1, \ldots, e_N\}$ be the class of rules, and assume that the teacher presents independent random examples, now subject to classification noise. To simplify the presentation, we shall assume that the identification procedure is told an upper bound $\eta_b < 1/2$ on the noise rate η (but not the actual rate, which could be much lower). Later we shall show that this assumption is not necessary.

The algorithm is a generalization of that in Example 4.6:

Algorithm 5.1 (Finite Pac-Identification)

INPUT:

- A finite class $\mathcal{E}$ of N rules.

- A computable test for agreement between an example and a rule.

- A probabilistic teacher EX_η, whose data may be subject to classification noise. (The noise rate η is not part of the input.)

- Fractions ϵ and δ, and η_b, with $0 < \epsilon, \delta \le 1/2$ and $0 \le \eta \le \eta_b < 1/2$.

OUTPUT:

A rule $e \in \mathcal{E}$.

PROCEDURE:

1. Request $m(\epsilon, \delta, N, \eta_b)$ examples. (The value of m is specified below.)

2. For each rule $e_i \in \mathcal{E}$, test e_i against all the examples and determine F_i, the number of *failures* (examples in disagreement with e_i).

3. Output any rule e with a minimum value for F_i, and halt.

$\diamond$

Let us now prove that this algorithm *pac*-identifies $\mathcal{E}$. In the proof to follow, we shall require the following inequality (a special case of Hoeffding's inequality, [30]). Consider a Bernoulli random variable with probability p of having the value 1 ("success", "heads"), and $1 - p$ of having value 0 ("tails"). Let $GE(p, m, r)$ be the probability of at least $\lceil rm \rceil$ successes in m independent trials, and $LE(p, m, r)$ the probability of at most $\lfloor rm \rfloor$ successes ($0 \le r \le 1$). The following lemma bounds the probability that r (the empirical rate of success) is very different from p.

Lemma 5.2 (Hoeffding's Inequality) If $0 \le p \le 1$, $0 \le s \le 1$, and m is any positive integer, then

$$LE(p, m, p - s) \le e^{-2s^2 m},$$

and

$$GE(p, m, p + s) \le e^{-2s^2 m}.$$

□

As an immediate corollary, if R denotes the total number of successes in m trials and $\hat{p} = R/m$, then

$$\Pr\left[|p - \hat{p}| \ge s\right] \le 2e^{-2s^2 m}.$$

Intuitively, these results imply that the probability the empirical rate of success $\hat{p}$ differs from the average rate p by s or more decreases exponentially with s^2 and with m. Thus with only a rather modest sample size m, we are able to estimate p accurately with high confidence.

In terms of the above algorithm, "success" for a rule e_i is the event of its disagreeing with a random example. In m examples, F_i is the number of "successes", and F_i/m is the empirical rate of disagreement, to be compared to its expected rate $p_{i,\eta}$.

Theorem 5.3 When

$$m \ge \frac{2}{\epsilon^2(1 - 2\eta_b)^2} \ln\left(\frac{2N}{\delta}\right), \tag{5.2}$$

Algorithm 5.1 pac-identifies $\mathcal{E}$.

PROOF: Recall Equation 5.1, and the subsequent discussion. The probability that a good rule fails on an example is η, while the probability that an ϵ-bad rule fails is at least $\eta + \epsilon(1 - 2\eta)$. The difference between these two rates is at least $\epsilon(1 - 2\eta) \ge \epsilon(1 - 2\eta_b) = s$.

The algorithm can go astray if some ϵ-bad rule happens to fail less often than all acceptable rules. Consider such an ϵ-bad rule e_i, and let

e_t be a correct rule (we know there is at least one). Let F_i and F_t be
their respective failure statistics. In order for e_i to be the result of the
algorithm, either

$$\frac{F_i}{m} \leq \eta + s/2$$

or

$$\frac{F_t}{m} \geq \eta + s/2,$$

or both. But this means that either F_i/m is less than its expected value
of $\eta + s$ by $s/2$, or F_t/m is greater than its expected value of η by $s/2$.
By Hoeffding's inequality above, the probability of the first of these is
at most

$$LE(\eta + s, m, \eta + s - s/2) \leq e^{-2(s/2)^2 m}$$
$$\leq \delta/2N.$$

Similarly, the latter is

$$GE(\eta, m, \eta + s/2) \leq \delta/2N.$$

Thus the probability that any particular ϵ-bad rule e_i fails less than e_t
is at most δ/N. Since there are fewer than N such bad rules, the total
probability that one of them minimizes the number of failures and is
output by the algorithm is less than δ.   □

The size m of the sample that we have computed in the preceding
analysis is not optimal; but it is polynomial in the appropriate quan-
tities: $1/\epsilon$, $1/\delta$, N, and $(1 - 2\eta_b)$. In particular, it depends on $(1/\epsilon)^2$,
whereas the corresponding estimate for noise-free data depends only on
$1/\epsilon$. A more careful analysis, using a different approach, is given in the
appendix to this chapter. It shows that the number of examples need

only increase as $1/\epsilon$. The analysis also provides a *lower* bound on the number of examples that grows as $1/(1-2\eta)$, showing that the actual asymptotic dependency on η is between $1/(1-2\eta)$ and $1/(1-2\eta)^2$, for error rates approaching $\frac{1}{2}$.

Comparison with Vapnik's result. Vapnik [74], whose work has been mentioned already, suggests a similar statistical approach when the examples are independently subjected to random classification errors that may depend on the content of the example. That is, instead of a uniform error rate η for all examples x drawn from P, the probability $\eta(x)$ of a classification error may depend upon the particular example x. Let e_0 be the hypothesis with the smallest expected rate of disagreement with the oracle EX_η; Vapnik shows that the sampling technique of Theorem 5.1 can be used to find (with probability at least $1-\delta$) a hypothesis e whose error $P[e \bigtriangleup e_0]$ relative to e_0 is at most ϵ.

With his procedure the intent is to discover the best rule for describing the sample data from a noisy source EX_η. By contrast, the intent of the above identification procedure is to discover the target rule underlying the data. These need not be the same; indeed, the rule e obtained with Vapnik's procedure may not have error at most ϵ, even when the mean rate of classification errors over the examples is less than one half. For example, let $\mathcal{E}$ represent subsets of $U = \{a, b\}$. Let the target be $e_t = \{a, b\}$, with examples distributed as follows: $P[a] = 0.1, P[b] = 0.9$, and $\eta(a) = 0.6, \eta(b) = 0.48$. Then the probability that e_t disagrees with a random example is $P[a]\eta(a) + P[b]\eta(b) = 0.492$, whereas the hypotheses $e_0 = \{b\}$ disagrees at a rate of $P[a](1 - \eta(a)) + P[b]\eta(b) = 0.472$. Thus e_0 fails on average less often than the correct set e_t, even though the mean rate of noise is 0.492 (less than half). So for this noise model, the algorithm may not choose an ϵ-good rule.

5.4.2 Infinite Classes

In the case of concept learning, we can extend this result to the identification of Vapnik-Chervonenkis (VC) classes, discussed in Section 4.2.3. These classes, recall, are precisely the concept-learning classes that can be *pac*-identified efficiently. Without excessive detail, we shall show how the preceding algorithm can be adapted. (Vapnik describes somewhat similar results in [74], but with a different model and a much more complex argument.)

Recall that, for concept learning, rules are representations for subsets of some universe U, and examples are elements of U. Recall also that we can think of each rule e as splitting a set S of examples into two subsets: those that are covered by the rule $(e \cap S)$ and those that are not $(S - e)$. The following discussion pertains to any rule class with finite dimension, including domains that may be uncountably infinite.

Our algorithm for identifying V-C classes depends upon two results from [15]. For the remainder of this section, $\mathcal{E}$ is a V-C class of dimension at most d.

Lemma 5.4 For any $S \subseteq U$ with at least d elements, $\mathcal{E}$ splits S in at most $|S|^d + 1$ ways.

Theorem 5.5 (from [15]) Fix $e_t \in \mathcal{E}$. There is a function[2] $m_1(\epsilon, \delta, d)$, polynomial in $1/\epsilon$, $\log 1/\delta$, and d, such that in a random sample of m_1

---

[2]The function is shown in Eq. (4.2).

examples drawn from P, with probability $\geq 1 - \delta$ at least one example is in each of the sets $e \bigtriangleup e_t$, uniformly for all ϵ-bad hypotheses e.

The idea behind the proof of Theorem 5.5 is that the m_1 examples are split by the hypotheses in $\mathcal{E}$ in at most $m_1{}^d + 1$ ways, so that even though $\mathcal{E}$ may be infinite, the rules can be grouped together into a finite set of equivalence classes according to how they split the examples. Let us call two hypotheses σ-*equivalent* if they split the sample σ into the same two subsets; this relation partitions $\mathcal{E}$ into a finite number of equivalence classes with respect to σ.

All hypotheses that are σ-equivalent to the target e_t will be consistent with σ. The value m_1 is shown to provide enough examples so that every ϵ-bad rule will disagree with at least one example, with probability at least $1 - \delta$, and thus will not be in the same σ-equivalence class with e_t.

Now imagine that we obtain the sample σ of size m_1 without the examples' being classified. The fact that σ partitions $\mathcal{E}$ into at most $m_1{}^d + 1$ equivalence classes still holds, as does the fact that with high probability at least one of these classes (the one containing e_t) consists of only ϵ-good hypotheses. Picking some representative hypothesis from each class, we have $m_1{}^d + 1$ candidates, at least one of which is ϵ-good with high probability.

Consider now how we might compensate for noise in this set σ of examples. Assume that η_b is given as an upper bound for the noise rate. There may be no candidate hypothesis consistent with this set of classified examples, so which one should we select? Guided by the results of the preceding section, we should probably choose the one with the smallest expected rate of disagreement. Before, when we were assured of having at least one rule that was correct, our statistics had to be able to distinguish a good rule from one that is ϵ-bad. Now, we shall use σ_1 to ensure that with high probability there is an $\epsilon/2$-good rule among the $N \leq m_1{}^d + 1$ candidates; and our statistics will distinguish this rule from one that is ϵ-bad. The minimum separation s between the expected rate of failure of an $\epsilon/2$-good rule and that of an ϵ-bad rule is only half of what it was in Algorithm 5.1. Thus the number of examples m_2 needed to test the N rules will be greater than the number required in that algorithm, and it may also be greater than m_1.

The algorithm below assumes that for the VC class $\mathcal{E}$ there is an algorithm that takes a set σ of examples and chooses a representative rule for each σ-equivalence class. For example, for the class I of open intervals on the real line R (Example 4.11), such a procedure might choose for each pair of points in the set one interval that includes that pair and all intervening points. In this case the $O(n^2)$ intervals are quickly chosen; but in general the existence and efficiency of such a procedure will depend on the domain.

The algorithm is as follows.

Algorithm 5.6 (Pac-identifying V-C Classes with Noise)

INPUT:

- A V-C class $\mathcal{E}$ of finite dimension d, with a procedure for choosing representative rules for σ-equivalence classes.
- A computable test for agreement between an example and a rule.

- A probabilistic teacher EX_η, whose data may be subject to classification noise. (The noise rate η is not part of the input.)

- Fractions ϵ, δ, and η_b, with $0 < \epsilon, \delta \leq 1/2$ and $0 \leq \eta \leq \eta_b < 1/2$.

OUTPUT:

A rule $e \in \mathcal{E}$.

PROCEDURE:

1. Request a sample σ_1 of size $m_1' \geq m_1(\epsilon/2, \delta/3, d)$, where m_1 is the polynomial promised by Theorem 5.5.

2. Select $\mathcal{E}_1 = \{e_1, \ldots, e_N\}$ as representatives of the σ_1-equivalence classes induced by σ_1, where $N \leq (m_1')^d + 1$.

3. Let σ_2 be the set of examples σ_1 with enough additional examples so that it contains at least

$$m_2 = \frac{2}{\left(\frac{\epsilon}{2}\right)^2 (1 - 2\eta_b)^2} \cdot \ln\left(\frac{2N}{\frac{2}{3}\delta}\right)$$

classified data points in all.

4. Output a hypothesis in $\mathcal{E}_1$ which minimizes the number of disagreements with σ_2.

Theorem 5.7 Algorithm 5.6 pac-identifies $\mathcal{E}$.

PROOF: By Theorem 5.5, $\mathcal{E}_1$ contains an $\epsilon/2$-good rule with probability at least $1 - (\delta/3)$. We claim that the rule e_i output by the algorithm is ϵ-good with probability at least $1 - \delta$.

For, if not, then at least one of the following must be true:

- Every hypothesis in $\mathcal{E}_1$ is $\epsilon/2$-bad. Let e be the rule in $\mathcal{E}_1$ that is σ_1-equivalent to e_t. Then there is no example in σ_1 that belongs to the set $e \triangle e_t$. But by Theorem 5.5 and the choice of m_1, the likelihood of this situation is less than $\delta/3$.

- For at least one ϵ-bad rule e_j in $\mathcal{E}_1$, the number of examples in σ_2 for which the rule e_j fails is at most $m_2(\eta + 3s/4)$, where $s = \epsilon(1 - 2\eta_b)$. But the expected rate of failure for e_j is at least $\eta + s$, and Hoeffding's Inequality (Lemma 5.2) bounds the probability of such a large deviation, $LE(\eta + s, m_2, \eta + 3s/4)$, by $\delta/3$.

- For every $\epsilon/2$-good rule e_i in $\mathcal{E}_1$, the number of examples in σ_2 for which e_i fails is at least $m_2(\eta + 3s/4)$. But the expected rate of failure for e_i is at most $\eta + s/2$, and Hoeffding's Inequality bounds the probability of such a large deviation, $GE(\eta + s/2, m_2, \eta + 3s/4)$, by $\delta/3$.

Thus the probability of any of these occurring is less than δ. $\qquad\square$

Since $m_1{}'$ is bounded by a polynomial in $1/\epsilon$ and $1/\delta$, so also are $\ln N$ and m_2, which are polynomially related to m_1.

As with error-free data, the problem of identification from more general examples than singleton sets is open.

5.4.3 Estimating the Noise Rate η

In the preceding results we have assumed that the identification procedure is told an upper bound on the noise rate η. We now show that this assumption is unnecessary.

Referring back to the "catalpa trees" example, our hero, who is struggling to learn from a fallible graduate assistant, is no longer assured that the assistant is wrong at most 45% of the time. Instead he assumes only that his teacher's error rate is less than 50%, and determines for himself an upper bound (indeed, an estimate) for the noise rate. The fact that this is possible is quite remarkable.

The description we give is for a finite class $\mathcal{E}$, but extends readily to Vapnik-Chervonenkis classes as well.

Here is the idea. Each rule in $\mathcal{E}$ has some probability of disagreeing with a (possibly noisy) example. With $\eta < 1/2$, the smallest probability is η itself, achieved by good rules. We want to find an upper bound (less than $1/2$) on this probability. Specifically, we seek a procedure which will output a value η_b, such that, with probability at least $1 - \delta/2$, η_b is between η and $1/2$. Given this value, we can use it in Algorithm 5.1, with $\delta/2$ replacing δ, to find an acceptable hypothesis with probability at least $1 - \delta/2$. The probability that either of these procedures fails is then $\leq \delta$.

The idea is to conduct a "binary search" for a value for η_b, starting with a guess of $1/4$, and if that value fails a test, try $3/8$, then $7/16$, etc. — each time, halving the distance between the previous guess and $1/2$. For the test, we draw some examples and estimate the failure probability of each of the rules in $\mathcal{E}$. The one with the smallest empirical failure rate $\hat{p}_i$ should satisfy the condition $\hat{p}_i < \eta_b$. If it does, we halt and output η_b as our bound. Otherwise we increase η_b and repeat, using a larger sample size with each iteration.

The specific algorithm is as follows:

Algorithm 5.8 (Estimating the Noise Rate)

INPUT:

- A finite class $\mathcal{E} = \{e_1, e_2, \ldots, e_N\}$.

- A fraction δ, specifying the confidence parameter.

- A probabilistic presentation for a target representable in $\mathcal{E}$, with classification noise at a rate less than $1/2$.

OUTPUT:

A fraction $\hat{\eta}_b$ representing an estimated upper bound for the noise rate η.

PROCEDURE:

1. Initialize $\hat{\eta}_b \leftarrow 1/4$ and $r \leftarrow 1$.

2. (Round r) Repeat until the halt condition is fulfilled:

    2.1 Request $m_r(N, \delta)$ examples. (The value of m_r is given below.)

    2.2 For each rule $e_i \in \mathcal{E}$, test e_i against all the examples and determine $\hat{p}_i = F_i / m_r$, the proportion of examples in disagreement with e_i. Let $\hat{p}_{\min}$ be the minimum such value.

    2.3 If $\hat{p}_{\min} < \hat{\eta}_b - 2^{-(r+2)}$, then halt and output $\hat{\eta}_b$.

    2.4 Else,

        2.41 $r \leftarrow r + 1$.

        2.42 $\hat{\eta}_b \leftarrow \frac{1}{2} - 2^{-(r+1)}$.

Theorem 5.9 Let

$$m_r(N, \delta) = 2^{2r+3} \cdot \ln\left(\frac{N2^{r+2}}{\delta}\right).$$

Then with probability at least $1 - \delta$, Algorithm 5.8 halts on or before round $r_0 = 1 + \lceil \log_2(1 - 2\eta)^{-1}\rceil$ and outputs an estimate $\hat{\eta}_b > \eta$.

PROOF: The value of m_r has been chosen so that in m_r examples of a rule with an expected failure rate of $p_{i,\eta}$,

$$\Pr\left[|\hat{p}_i - p_{i,\eta}| \geq 2^{-(r+2)}\right] \leq \frac{(\delta/2)}{N2^r},$$

as one can check with Hoeffding's Inequality. After we have summed over all N rules and over all rounds $r \geq 1$, the probability that in any round the empirical value $\hat{p}_i$ for some rule deviates from its expected value $p_{i,\eta}$ by as much as $2^{-(r+2)}$ is less than $\delta/2$.

We claim that, with probability at least $1 - \delta/2$,

- the algorithm halts on or before round $r_0 = 1 + \lceil \log_2(1 - 2\eta)^{-1}\rceil$.
- when it halts, $\hat{\eta}_b > \eta$.

In round r_0, $\eta \leq \frac{1}{2} - 1/2^{r_0}$, and m_{r_0} is sufficient to ensure that $\hat{p}_{\min} \leq \eta + 2^{-(r_0+2)}$, with probability at least $1 - \delta/2$. But

$$
\begin{aligned}
\hat{\eta}_b - 2^{-(r_0+2)} &= \left(\frac{1}{2} - \frac{1}{2^{r_0+1}}\right) - \frac{1}{2^{r_0+2}} \\
&> \left(\frac{1}{2} - \frac{1}{2^{r_0}}\right) - \frac{1}{2^{r_0+2}} \\
&\geq \eta + 2^{-(r_0+2)} \\
&\geq \hat{p}_{\min}.
\end{aligned}
$$

with probability at least $1 - \delta/2$. Thus the algorithm will halt at or before round r_0 with this probability.

Suppose the algorithm halts in round r. By choice of m_r, $\hat{p}_{\min} \geq \eta - 2^{-(r+2)}$ with probability at least $1 - \delta/2$. The fact that it stops implies that $\hat{p}_{\min} < \hat{\eta}_b - 2^{-(r+2)}$. Thus

$$\eta - \frac{1}{2^{r+2}} < \hat{\eta}_b - \frac{1}{2^{r+2}},$$

and hence $\eta < \hat{\eta}_b$ with probability at least $1 - \delta/2$.

Finally, the algorithm fails only if at least one of the above two conditions fails. Since each occurs with probability less than $\delta/2$, failure occurs with probability less than δ. $\square$

Some things to note: With probability zero, the algorithm could fail to halt. Thus strictly speaking, it is not a finite procedure. Assuming it halts in round $r_0 = 1 + \lceil \log_2(1 - 2\eta)^{-1} \rceil$, the total number of examples required is $\mathcal{O}((1 - 2\eta)^{-2} \cdot \ln[N/(1 - 2\eta)\delta])$. Thus aymptotically the process of determining η_b increases the sample size only slightly.

Also, we can accelerate the convergence by allowing $\hat{\eta}_b$ in each round to be the larger of the value obtained in step 2.42 and $\hat{p}_{\min}$.

Finally, it is not difficult to integrate Algorithms 5.1 and 5.8 into a single algorithm which uses the m_r examples from the final round to select a hypothesis.

5.5   Probabilistic Identification in the Limit

In Section 4.1 an algorithm was given for identification in the limit from a probabilistic teacher. The algorithm identified, with probability one, a rule e whose error $P(e \bigtriangleup e_t)$ with respect to the target e_t is zero. Let us extend this result to the case where example data may suffer classification noise, with parameter η. The algorithm is interesting because it works for any domain, not just those with finite dimension.

Algorithm 4.2 is highly dependent on noise-free examples because a single noise example could cause it to reject the only correct rule. Consider how we need to modify the algorithm. Clearly we cannot reject any rule e permanently just because it has a counterexample. Instead, we shall maintain statistics on the rate of failure for each rule, and tend to prefer the rule(s) with the smallest failure rate.

On the other hand, there may be several correct rules, and statistical fluctuations will cause the empirical failure rates of these rules to vary. Since no one rule can be expected to have the smallest rate of failure forever, we may change preferences endlessly back and forth among the various correct rules if we always output the rule with the smallest rate of failure.

Our solution to these problems is to keep all the possible rules on a queue, to which we add one new rule in the list $\mathcal{E}$ on each round r of the algorithm. The rule e_{front} at the front of the queue is the current guess. We will count the number of disagreements with the examples for each rule and compute its empirical rate of failure $\hat{p}$.

But before we replace e_{front} by the rule $e_{\min}$ with the smallest failure rate $\hat{p}$, we require that the failure rates differ by more than some "damping" interval I_r: this will prevent one correct rule from replacing another more than finitely often.

By letting I_r decrease slowly to 0 as $r \to \infty$, we ensure (by the Law of Large Numbers) that any incorrect rule will eventually be displaced. When e_{front} is replaced, the queue is rotated: rules at the front of the

queue are popped and requeued to the back, until the rule at the front
has a failure rate no larger than that of e_{min} plus the damping interval.
The essential feature provided by the queue structure is *fairness*: every
rule has infinitely many opportunities to reach the front of the queue
and become the current hypothesis.

In the following, let

$$I_r = \sqrt{\frac{\log_2 r}{r}}$$

and

$$m_r = \frac{\ln(r2^r)}{2I_r^2}.$$

Algorithm 5.10 (Stochastic Infinite Identification)

INPUT:

- An r.e. class $\mathcal{E} = \{e_1, e_2, \ldots\}$.
- A probabilistic presentation for a target representable in $\mathcal{E}$, with
  classification noise at a rate less than $1/2$.

OUTPUT:

An infinite sequence $H_1, \ldots$ of rules in $\mathcal{E}$

PROCEDURE:

1. $Q \leftarrow empty$. $r \leftarrow 0$.

2. For $r \leftarrow 1$ to ∞, do (round r):

   2.1 Enqueue e_r (at the end of Q). Let $Q = \langle q_1, \ldots, q_r \rangle$, where
   each q_i is one of the first r rules in $\mathcal{E}$, q_r is e_r, and q_1 is the
   "current" favorite hypothesis.

2.2 Request m_r examples, and test each rule in Q against each example. Let $\hat{p}_i$ be the fraction of examples with which rule q_i disagrees $(1 \leq i \leq r)$.

2.3 Let $\hat{p}_{\min}$ be the smallest failure rate, and $q_{\min}$ the rule nearest the front of Q achieving that rate. If $\hat{p}_{\min} < \hat{p}_1 - 2I_r$, then rotate the queue front to back until the rule e_1 at the front satisfies the condition $\hat{p}_{\min} \geq \hat{p}_1 - 2I_r$.

2.4 Output the rule at the front of the queue.

$\diamond$

Theorem 5.11 Algorithm 5.10 stochastically identifies $\mathcal{E}$ in the limit.

PROOF: The algorithm can fail in two ways: by converging to a rule with non-zero error, or by changing its mind infinitely often.

Suppose it converges to a rule e_i whose error $p_i > 0$. Consider only those rounds after the one on which a correct rule e_t is added to the queue. Let $p_{i,\eta}$ and $p_{t,\eta}$ denote, respectively, the expected probabilities that these two rules will disagree with a random example, in the presence of a classification noise rate of η.

Recall that $p_{i,\eta} > p_{t,\eta} = \eta$. Since $I_r \to 0$, there exists a round r_0 such that for all $r \geq r_0$, $I_r < (p_{i,\eta} - \eta)/4$. Consider those rounds for which this condition holds. Clearly the probability that e_i is never discarded after round r_0 is no greater than the probability that the particular rule e_t never displaces e_i after round r_0. Let E_r be the event: e_i is *not* displaced by e_t in round r. We claim that $\sum_{r=r_0}^{\infty} \Pr[E_r]$ is finite; by the Borel-Cantelli Lemma (Lemma 4.4) we may then conclude that e_i is ultimately rejected with probability one.

To prove the claim, let $\hat{p}_i$ and $\hat{p}_t$ be the empirical failure rates of the rules on the r'th round. E_r occurs if $\hat{p}_t + I_r \geq \hat{p}_i - I_r$. Since by assumption $p_{i,\eta} - p_{t,\eta} \geq 4I_r$, this can occur only if either $\hat{p}_t - p_{t,\eta} > I_r$ or $p_{i,\eta} - \hat{p}_i > I_r$, or both. Thus

$$\Pr[E_r] \leq LE(p_{i,\eta}, m_r, p_{i,\eta} - I_r) + GE(p_{t,\eta}, m_r, p_{t,\eta} + I_r).$$

By Hoeffding's Inequality (Lemma 5.2), with the value m_r as stated in the theorem,

$$\Pr[E_r] \leq 2e^{-2m_r I_r{}^2}$$
$$< \frac{2}{r2^r}.$$

Summing this for $r \geq r_0$ completes the proof of the claim.

Now suppose the algorithm vacillates infinitely often. Again consider those rounds occurring after some correct rule e_t has been enqueued. Call the r'th round a "displacement event for t" $D_r(t)$ if there exists a rule e_i on the queue such that $\hat{p}_i < \hat{p}_t + 2I_r$ — i.e., , should e_t be at the front of queue, it will be displaced by some hypothesis e_i. By the Law of the Iterated Logarithm (e.g., [23]), there is, with probability one, a round r_0 such that, for all rounds $r \geq r_0$, $|\hat{p}_t - \eta| < I_r$. We claim that $\sum_{r \geq r_0} \Pr[D_r(t)]$ is finite, and hence only finitely many of the events $D_r(t)$ occur, with probability one. It also follows that e_t is not rotated infinitely often from the front of the queue (again, with probability one). But if the identification algorithm never converges, e_t will have to be rotated from the front infinitely often. We conclude that the algorithm must converge, if not to e_t, then to some other rule with zero error.

To prove the claim, suppose $r \geq r_0$ and that e_i displaces e_t. Since $p_{i,\eta} > p_{t,\eta} = \eta$ and (by definition of r_0) $\hat{p}_t \leq \eta + I_r$, it must be the case that $\hat{p}_i \leq \eta - I_r$. But by Hoeffding's inequality, with a sample size of m_r, the probability of this is $\leq \exp[-2m_r I_r^2] = 1/(r2^r)$. Since there are fewer than r hypotheses on the queue to challenge e_t, the total probability of the displacement event $D_r(t)$ is bounded by $1/2^r$. These probabilities sum to at most one.   □

Note that $m_r = O(r^2)$. Also, the proof does not require that m_r fresh examples be drawn on every round, but only that there be m_r independent examples available in round r; thus examples from previous rounds may be reused.

A weakness of this algorithm, not present in the noise-free version, is that an ever-larger set of rules must be tested on each round. In this sense the algorithm is non-incremental. Discovery of an incremental algorithm is suggested as an interesting problem.

5.6   Identifying Normal-Form Expressions

In Section 4.2.2 we saw how to pac-identify families $\mathcal{E}_n$ of ⊙-normal form rules efficiently, assuming that the number of components in each family grows as a polynomial in n and that components can be tested efficiently for agreement with the examples. Let us consider the same problem[3] in the presence of classification noise.

---

[3]Dual statements applying to ⊕-normal forms are omitted.

Algorithm 5.1 certainly solves the problem effectively; and the size of the sample data required is polynomial in $1/\epsilon$, $\log 1/\delta$, $1/(1 - 2\eta_b)$, and $\log N$ where $N = \mathcal{O}(2^{n^b})$ for some constant b. But the algorithm requires that we search all the rules for one with the fewest disagreements. Given that there may be exponentially many rules associated with only polynomially many components, we may ask whether this can be done in time polynomial in n.

In general, it probably cannot. A theorem, due to Angluin and proved in [6], shows that for the class of $CNF_n(k)$ rules, even when the rules are limited to a very special subset with only 2^n rules, the problem of deciding whether one of the rules has fewer than d disagreements for a given sequence σ of examples is NP-complete.

This is discouraging, but not hopeless. Note that the strategy of minimizing disagreements is only one way of achieving the actual goal of pac-identification (finding a rule with error at most ϵ). Nothing requires that the rule be the best possible. *The purpose of this section is to show that other strategies are also possible.*

The question we consider is this one: can $\odot$-normal form rules be pac-identified efficiently with classification noise? We shall show that they can indeed. And as with Algorithm 4.9, the idea is to test components, not rules, for agreement with the examples.

Main ideas. Because the details of the algorithm and its analysis are rather involved, let us begin with an intuitive overview of the main ideas. Let M be the number of components (assumed to be a polynomial in n). As before, there are two ways we can go wrong: we can make an error of commission by including a *harmful* component that renders the expression too specific; or we can make an error of omission by failing to include an *important* component, and rendering the expression too general.

Recall the key feature of $\odot$-normal form expressions, that if component c fails to cover an example x, then no expression $c \odot e$ with c as a component will cover x either. Suppose that we are able to include every component c_i correct[4] for the target e_t and for which the probability of drawing a valid negative example not covered by c is $\epsilon/2M$ or more. Then even if we should omit all of the remaining correct components, the total error (of omission) is at most $\epsilon/2$.

Similarly, if we correctly exclude any incorrect component that fails to cover a valid positive example with probability $\epsilon/2M$ or more, then including all the remaining incorrect components can bring an error of at most $\epsilon/2$. By achieving both goals, we shall obtain a rule with error at most ϵ.

The strategy, then, is to determine which components have significant probability of disagreeing with an example x (whether that example is classified as positive or negative), and then eliminating those components which are not correct for the target rule e_t. Since there are exponentially fewer components than $\odot$-normal form expressions, such a strategy may be feasible even when one for testing the expressions themselves is not.

The algorithm we develop is theoretically feasible in that the computation time is polynomial in the appropriate quantities, including

---

[4]Recall Def. 3.17, that c is correct for e_t if $h(c \odot e_t) = h(e_t)$.

M. But like Algorithm 4.9 it cannot be viewed as practical for concept-learning applications, even when the number of attributes is fairly modest, because the constants are large and the number of examples is polynomial in the total number of attributes. But in addition to being theoretically interesting, it shows how we can make use of syntactical properties of the rules to find an acceptable hypothesis more quickly than with blind search.

The presentation to follow is rather technical; casual readers may wish to omit the remainder of this section.

Notation. Let the components be $c_1, \ldots, c_M$. Consider for the moment the content of the examples from EX_η, ignoring their classification as positive or negative. If an example x is not covered by a component c_i — i.e., $GE?(c_i, x) = no$, then we write $c_i(x) = 0$; otherwise we write $c_i(x) = 1$. Let $p_0(c)$ be the probability that an example x is drawn such that $c(x) = 0$. The complementary probability is $p_1(c) = 1 - p_0(c)$.

Of the examples not covered by c, some may agree with the target e_t and some may not. Let $p_{01}(c)$ be the probability of receiving an example x such that $c(x) = 0$ but $e_t(x) = 1$. Similarly, $p_{00}(c)$ is the probability that $c(x) = 0$ and $e_t(x) = 0$. Clearly $p_{00}(c) + p_{01}(c) = p_0(c)$.

Since the learner doesn't know e_t, $p_{00}(c)$ and $p_{01}(c)$ cannot be measured directly. However, we can estimate $p_{0+}(c)$, the probability of drawing a positive example for which $c(x) = 0$. For very low noise rates, $p_{0+}(c)$ and $p_{01}(c)$ will be nearly equal. See Figure 5.1 for a summary of the notation.

NOTATION SUMMARY	
QUANTITY	INTERPRETATION: probability of drawing an example such that...
$p_0(c)$	$c(x) = 0$
$p_1(c)$	$c(x) = 1$
$p_{00}(c)$	$c(x) = 0, e_t(x) = 0$
$p_{01}(c)$	$c(x) = 0, e_t(x) = 1$
$p_{0+}(c)$	$c(x) = 0, x$ is a positive example
p_-	x is a negative example

Figure 5.1: Notation Summary.

The "Choosy" Lemma. Components c for which $p_0(c)$ is big will have a big effect if included in the rule. We therefore make the following definition:

Definition 5.12 A component c is said to be *important* if $p_0(c) \geq Q_I$, where $Q_I = \epsilon/16M^2$.

Since $p_0(c)$ depends only on the content of the examples, it can be estimated for each component by random sampling: draw some examples, and (ignoring the signs) determine the fraction for which $c(x) = 0$. If c is correct (for e_t), then $p_0(c) = p_{00}(c)$. Otherwise, there may be examples x for which $c(x) = 0$ but $e_t(x) = 1$. When this likelihood is significant, the component is *harmful*.

Definition 5.13 A component c is said to be *harmful* if $p_{01}(c) \geq Q_H$, where $Q_H = \epsilon/2M$. Note that every harmful component is also important, since $Q_H > Q_I$.

How can we detect the harmful components from among the important ones? We can't directly: because of classification noise, some examples x may be presented as positive for which $e_t(x) = 0$. The task of the algorithm is to distinguish the harmful components by sampling. We shall find that, among the important components, the harmful ones are contradicted more often by positive examples than are the correct ones. This fact is the basis for the algorithm below.

Lemma 5.14 ("Choosy") Let e be any $\odot$-normal form rule that includes all important components that are not harmful. Then the error of e is less than ϵ.

PROOF: Let e_t be the target rule, and e any $\odot$-normal form expression. Let $e - e_t$ be the set of components correct for e that are not correct for e_t, and vice versa for $e_t - e$. By assumption $e - e_t$ contains no harmful components, while $e_t - e$ contains no important ones.

We can bound the error $P(e \triangle e_t)$ of e as follows. The probability of drawing an example in $e_t \triangle e$ has two parts:

- The example could agree with e_t but not with e. The probability of this is bounded by

$$\sum_{c \in e - e_t} p_{01}(c) \; < \; MQ_H, \text{ since no element of } e - e_t \text{ is harmful,}$$

$$< \; \epsilon/2.$$

- The example could agree with e but not with e_t. The probability of this is bounded by

$$\sum_{c \in e_t - e} p_0(c) \; < \; MQ_I, \text{ since no element of } e_t - e \text{ is important,}$$

$$< \quad \epsilon/2.$$

Together the likelihood of these is $< \epsilon$.   □

Finding the harmful components. Since we cannot measure $p_{01}(c)$ directly, we need an indirect way to estimate it. What we *can* measure are $p_0(c)$ and $p_{0+}(c)$. The next lemma says that the ratio of these two probabilities separates the harmful from the correct components.

Lemma 5.15 Assume the examples are subject to classification noise with probability $\eta < 1/2$. Let c_h be a harmful component and c_c a correct component. Then, provided $p_0(c_c) > 0$,

$$\frac{p_{0+}(c_h)}{p_0(c_h)} \geq \frac{p_{0+}(c_c)}{p_0(c_c)} + s,$$

where $s = Q_H(1 - 2\eta)$.

PROOF: For any component c, $p_{0+}(c)$ can be calculated as follows:

$$
\begin{aligned}
p_{0+}(c) &= (1 - \eta)p_{01}(c) + \eta p_{00}(c) \\
&= \eta(p_{00}(c) + p_{01}(c)) + (1 - 2\eta)p_{01}(c) \\
&= \eta p_0(c) + (1 - 2\eta)p_{01}(c).
\end{aligned}
$$

If $p_0(c) \neq 0$ then

$$\frac{p_{0+}(c)}{p_0(c)} = \eta + \frac{p_{01}(c)}{p_0(c)}(1 - 2\eta). \tag{5.3}$$

Since $\eta < 1/2$, this quantity is always greater than or equal to η; and if c is correct, $p_{01}(c) = 0$, so this quantity is equal to η. Clearly $p_0(c) \leq 1$, for all component c such that $p_0(c) \neq 0$, and so

$$\frac{p_{0+}(c)}{p_0(c)} \geq \eta + p_{01}(c)(1 - 2\eta). \tag{5.4}$$

If c_h is a harmful component, then $p_{01}(c_h) \geq Q_H$. Therefore

$$\frac{p_{0+}(c_h)}{p_0(c_h)} \geq \eta + Q_H(1 - 2\eta).$$

Thus between c_h and c_c, the ratio $p_{0+}(c)/p_0(c)$ differs by at least s.

$\square$

The quantity $s = Q_H(1-2\eta)$ gives the statistical separation between harmful and correct components, just as $\epsilon(1-2\eta)$ separates correct and ϵ-bad rules in Algorithm 5.1.

Our algorithm has two parts:

1. Determine the important components.
2. Use Lemma 5.15 to eliminate the harmful components.

Provided we can accomplish these with high probability, the "Choosy Lemma" assures us that the remaining components together form an $\odot$-normal form rule with small enough error to satisfy the requirements of pac-identification.

The Algorithm. As with Algorithm 5.1, we shall first assume that an upper bound η_b is given such that $\eta \leq \eta_b < \frac{1}{2}$. Subsequently we remove this assumption.

Algorithm 5.16 (Efficient Normal Form Identification)

INPUT:

- A finite class $\mathcal{E}$ with an $\odot$-normal form property, with a set of M components $c_1, \ldots, c_M$ and a most-general expression $\top$.

- Positive fractions ϵ and δ, and a bound η_b, all $< \frac{1}{2}$.

- Oracles GE? and EX_η.

OUTPUT:

An $\odot$-normal form rule $e \in \mathcal{E}$.

PROCEDURE:

1. Compute $Q_H = \epsilon/2M$, $Q_I = \epsilon/16M^2$, and $s_b = Q_H(1 - 2\eta_b)$.

2. Request $m(\epsilon, \delta, M, \eta_b)$ examples. (The value of m is given below.)

3. Test each component c and for each compute

    3.1 $\hat{p}_0(c)$, the fraction of examples x such that $c(x) = 0$.

    3.2 $\hat{p}_{0+}(c)$, the fraction of examples x which are positive and are such that $c(x) = 0$.

4. Also, compute $\hat{p}_-$, the fraction of examples classified as negative.

5. (Select important components:) Let $I =$ the set of all components c such that $\hat{p}_0(c) \geq Q_I/2$.

6. (Estimate η:) Let $\hat{\eta}_1 = \hat{p}_-$.
    Let $\hat{\eta}_2 = \min\{\hat{p}_{0+}(c)/\hat{p}_0(c) \mid c \in I\}$.
    Set $\hat{\eta} = \min[\hat{\eta}_1, \hat{\eta}_2]$.

7. (Discard harmful components) Remove from I all components c such that $\hat{p}_{0+}(c)/\hat{p}_0(c) > \hat{\eta} + s_b/2$.

8. Output the expression consisting of all remaining components in I conjoined by $\odot$, or $\top$ in case I is empty. ◇

Theorem 5.17 When

$$m \geq \frac{2^{10} M^4}{\epsilon^3 (1 - 2\eta_b)^2} \ln \left(\frac{6M}{\delta} \right),$$

Algorithm 5.16 pac-identifies $\mathcal{E}$ in $\odot$-normal form.

The main corollary is

Corollary 5.18 For fixed k, the family $CNF_n(k)$ can be pac-identified in time polynomial in n, $1/\epsilon$, $\ln(1/\delta)$, and $1/(1 - 2\eta_b)$ when examples consist of truth-value assignments to each of the n variables.

(Because, the number of clauses M is polynomial in n, each clause can be tested efficiently, and the sample size m is polynomial in the relevant parameters.)

PROOF: Consider how the algorithm could go astray:

- Some important component might not be selected for inclusion in I.

- The estimate $\hat{\eta}$ could be too large or too small.

- Some harmful component could enjoy an abnormally small number of failures on positive examples and thereby be included in the output expression.

- Some correct component could suffer an abnormally large proportion of failures on positive examples and thereby be excluded from the output expression.

The series of lemmas below shows that the second possibility has probability less than $\delta/2$, while the others each have probability at most $\delta/6$. In all, therefore, these mishaps have probability less than δ, and by the Choosy Lemma, the output expression will be ϵ-good with high probability. $\square$

In the following technical lemmas, "with high probability" (w.h.p.) means "with probability $\geq 1 - \delta/6$".

Lemma 5.19 After step 5 of the algorithm, the set I includes w.h.p. all components c such that $p_0(c) \geq Q_I$.

PROOF: For an important component c to be omitted, its empirical value $\hat{p}_0(c)$ must be less than $Q_I/2$ – an amount more than $Q_I/2$ below its expected value. With the sample size m given in the theorem, Hoeffding's Inequality (Lemma 5.2) shows that $LE(p_0(c), m, Q_I/2) < \delta/6M$. Summing this probability over M components completes the proof. $\square$

Lemma 5.20 Let $s = Q_H(1 - 2\eta)$. Then $\hat{\eta}_1 \geq \eta - s/4$ w.h.p.

PROOF: Consider the probability p_- that an example is classified negative by the noisy oracle. Without noise this probability is $p_0(e_t)$ (e_t is the target rule). With noise, this probability becomes

$$
\begin{aligned}
p_- &= (1 - \eta)p_0(e_t) + \eta(1 - p_0(e_t)) \\
&= \eta + p_0(e_t)(1 - 2\eta) \qquad\qquad (5.5) \\
&\geq \eta.
\end{aligned}
$$

By Hoeffding's Inequality, $LE(\eta, m, \eta - s/4) \leq LE(\eta, m, \eta - s_b/4) < \delta/6$.

□

Lemma 5.21 Given that I contains all important components, $\hat{\eta}_2 \geq \eta - s/4$ w.h.p.

PROOF: $\hat{\eta}_2$ will be too small iff, for some component c,

$$\frac{\hat{p}_{0+}(c)}{\hat{p}_0(c)} < \eta - s/4.$$

But by Eq. (5.4) $p_{0+}(c)/p_0(c)$ is $\geq \eta$. The sample size over which the ratio is being measured is at least $mQ_I/2$ since $c \in I$. Using Hoeffding's Inequality, $LE(\eta, mQ_I/2, \eta - s/4) \leq LE(\eta, mQ_I/2, \eta - s_b/4) \leq \delta/6M$. Summing this probability over all M components completes the proof.
□

Lemma 5.22 Given that I contains all important components, then w.h.p. either $\hat{\eta}_1 \leq \eta + s/4$ or $\hat{\eta}_2 \leq \eta + s/4$. Thus $\hat{\eta} \leq \eta + s/4$.

PROOF: There are two cases.

CASE: There is a component c in I that is correct for e_t. Then

$$\frac{p_{0+}(c)}{p_0(c)} = \eta$$

by Eq. (5.3). By Hoeffding's Inequality, $LE(\eta, mQ_I/2, \eta + s_b/4) \leq \delta/6$. Thus $\hat{\eta}_2 \leq \eta + s/4$ w.h.p.

CASE: There is no component c in I that is correct for e_t. $\hat{\eta}_1$ estimates p_-, and by Eq. (5.5) p_- depends on $p_0(e_t)$. We can bound the latter as follows:

$$p_0(e_t) \leq \sum_{c \in e_t} p_0(c),$$

$$< \sum_{c \in e_t} Q_I, \text{ since no component in } e_t \text{ is important,}$$

$$< MQ_I,$$

$$= Q_H/8.$$

Thus $p_- < \eta + Q_H(1 - 2\eta)/8 = \eta + s/8$, and by Hoeffding's Inequality, $GE(\eta + s/8, m, \eta + s/4) \le GE(\eta + s/8, m, \eta + s/8 + s_b/8) < \delta/6$. Hence $\hat{\eta}_1 \le \eta + s/4$ w.h.p. $\square$

Lemma 5.23 Given that I contains all important components, with probability $\ge 1 - \delta/2$, $|\hat{\eta} - \eta| \le s/4$.

PROOF: Immediate from Lemmas 5.20–5.22. $\square$

Lemma 5.24 Given that I contains all important components and that $|\hat{\eta} - \eta| \le s/4$, every harmful component is discarded w.h.p.

PROOF: A harmful component c is included if

$$\frac{\hat{p}_{0+}(c)}{\hat{p}_0(c)} \le \hat{\eta} + s_b/2.$$

And given that $\hat{\eta} \le \eta + s/4$, it certainly must be the case that

$$\frac{\hat{p}_{0+}(c)}{\hat{p}_0(c)} \le \eta + 3s/4$$

if the component is to be included.

But for such a component this ratio has an expected value of at least $\eta + s$. To be included, it must therefore deviate from its expected value by at least $s/4$, in a sample of at least $mQ_I/2$ positive examples. And $LE(\eta + s, mQ_I/2, \eta + 3s/4) \le LE(\eta + s, mQ_I/2, \eta + 3s_b/4) \le \delta/6M$. Summing this probability over possibly M harmful components yields the result. $\square$

Lemma 5.25 Given that I contains all important components and that $|\hat{\eta} - \eta| < s/4$, w.h.p. no correct important component is discarded.

PROOF: For a correct component, $p_{0+}(c)/p_0(c) = \eta$, and it will be discarded only if the empirical value of this ratio exceeds η by more than $s_b/4$. Hoeffding's Inequality shows that this probability is $< \delta/6M$. Summing over possibly M correct components yields the result.   □

Estimating the noise rate. If η_b is not given, we can deduce it with high probability from the data, using the same idea as that in Section 5.4.3. Initially we guess a bound of $\eta_b = 1/4$ and run steps 1 – 6 of the algorithm. The result is an estimate for $\hat{\eta}$, which should be less than η_b. If not, we increase our guess to $3/8$ and repeat the procedure. (And so on.) To allow for statistical fluctuation, the sample size m will increase slightly in each round.

For the sake of completeness, the details are sketched below.

Algorithm 5.26 (Estimating the Noise Rate)

INPUT:

- A finite class $\mathcal{E}$ with an $\odot$-normal form property, including a set of M components $c_1, \ldots, c_M$ and a most-general expression $\top$.
- Positive fractions ϵ and $\delta < \frac{1}{2}$.
- Oracles $GE?$ and EX_η.

OUTPUT:

An $\odot$-normal form rule $e \in \mathcal{E}$.

PROCEDURE:

1. Compute $Q_H = \epsilon/2M$, and $Q_I = \epsilon/16M^2$.

2. For $r = 1, 2, \ldots$ until the halt condition is satisfied: (Round r)

   2.1 Let $\hat{\eta}_b = \frac{1}{2} - 2^{-(r+1)}$.

   2.2 Request
   $$m_r = \frac{2^{10} M^4}{\epsilon^3 (1 - 2\eta_b)^2} \ln \left(2^r \cdot \frac{6M}{\delta} \right)$$
   examples.

   2.3 Test each component c and for each compute

   2.31 $\hat{p}_0(c)$, the fraction of examples x such that $c(x) = 0$.

   2.32 $\hat{p}_{0+}$, the fraction of examples x which are positive and are such that $c(x) = 0$.

   2.4 Also, compute $\hat{p}_-$, the fraction of examples classified as negative.

2.5 (Select important components:) Let $I =$ the set of all components c such that $\hat{p}_0(c) \geq Q_I/2$.

2.6 (Estimate η:) Let $\hat{\eta}_1 = \hat{p}_-$.
Let $\hat{\eta}_2 = \min\{\hat{p}_{0+}(c)/\hat{p}_0(c) \mid c \in I\}$.
Set $\hat{\eta} = \min[\hat{\eta}_1, \hat{\eta}_2]$.

2.7 If $\hat{\eta} < \hat{\eta}_b - 2^{-(r+2)}$, halt and output $\hat{\eta}_b$.

2.8 Else next round.

$\diamond$

Theorem 5.27 With probability at least $1 - \delta$, Algorithm 5.26 halts on or before round $r_0 = 1 + \lceil \log_2(1 - 2\eta)^{-1} \rceil$ and outputs a value $\hat{\eta}_b$ such that $\hat{\eta}_b > \eta$.

PROOF: The proof has two parts. First, we show that the algorithm halts on or before round $r_0 = 1 + \lceil \log_2(1 - 2\eta)^{-1} \rceil$. The analysis of Theorem 5.17 can be carried through to show that, with a sample size of m_r, $|\hat{\eta} - \eta| \leq s/4 = Q_H(1 - 2\eta)/4$ after this round with probability at least $1 - \delta 2^{-(r_0+1)}$. Thus with at least this probability,

$$
\begin{aligned}
\hat{\eta} &\leq \eta + s/4 \\
&= \eta + \frac{\epsilon(1 - 2\eta)}{8M} \\
&< \eta + \frac{1 - 2\eta}{8} \\
&= \frac{1}{8} + \frac{3\eta}{4}
\end{aligned}
$$

And since $\eta \leq \frac{1}{2} - 2^{-r_0}$, this is

$$
\leq \frac{1}{2} - \frac{3}{4} \cdot 2^{-r_0}
$$

$$= \hat{\eta}_b - 2^{-(r_0+2)}$$

since $\hat{\eta}_b = \frac{1}{2} - 2^{-(r_0+1)}$. Hence the algorithm halts in round r_0 with probability at least $1 - \delta/4$.

Next, assuming it halts in round r, we show that $\hat{\eta}_b \geq \eta$ with high probability. The halting condition is $\hat{\eta} < \hat{\eta}_b - 2^{-(r+2)}$. Let $\hat{s}_b = Q_H(1 - 2\hat{\eta}_b)$; After step 2.6, the analysis of Theorem 5.17 can be carried through, with the sample size given by m_r, to show that with probability at least $1 - \delta 2^{-(r+1)}$, the estimate $\hat{\eta}$ is at most $\hat{s}_b/4$ below its expected value η. Thus

$$
\begin{aligned}
\hat{\eta} &\geq \eta - \hat{s}_b/4 \\
&= \eta - \frac{\epsilon(1 - 2\hat{\eta}_b)}{8M} \\
&\geq \eta - \frac{1 - 2\hat{\eta}_b}{4} \\
&= \eta - 2^{-(r+2)},
\end{aligned}
$$

after substituting $\hat{\eta}_b = \frac{1}{2} - 2^{-(r+1)}$. Combining the two inequalities for $\hat{\eta}$, we have $\eta_b > \eta$, with probability at least $1 - \delta 2^{-(r+1)}$. Summing over all rounds r shows that this holds with probability at least $1 - \delta/2$. Since the algorithm fails only if it either fails to halt or it outputs a bad value, we conclude that the algorithm fails with probability less than $\delta/4 + \delta/2 < \delta$. $\square$

In practice, Algorithms 5.26 and 5.16 would be integrated into a single algorithm.

5.7   Other Models of Noise

Our model of random noise allows that some noise process may affect the example after selection and classification but before presentation to the learner. So far the only noise process we have studied is the Classification Noise Process (CNP). But what happens when a different noise process is at work? How do the algorithms and the theory change? For clarity, we shall discuss only the case of a finite concept-learning class (i.e., subsets of a finite set U), but the ideas can be applied more generally.

The results of this section show that the ideas presented so far are not specific to just one particular type of noise. The more we know about the noise process and its statistics, the better we can adjust our algorithms to handle it. Knowing nothing, we must assume an adversarial-type (worst-case) situation. With more information, we may be able to use a more general model such as the Bernoulli process.

Adversarial Noise.   First, we imagine a "worst-case" noise process, one which may substitute the most damaging example, from the learner's perspective. The questions we want to answer are:

- How much noise can we tolerate without destroying our ability to pac-identify the class?

- What algorithm do we use to overcome this type of noise?

The answers, in qualitative terms are: Considerably less noise can be tolerated than with the CNP; and yet the same basic algorithm applies.

Definition 5.28 In an *Adversarial Noise Process* (ANP), each example is replaced independently, with probability η, by an arbitrary example, possibly maliciously chosen.

Since the ANP subsumes the CNP, the maximum tolerable noise rate is certainly less than $1/2$. In fact, a simple argument shows that *pac-identification is possible provided* $\eta < \epsilon/(1 + \epsilon)$ (somewhat less than ϵ), and need not be possible otherwise. (Note that, unlike the CNP, this limit depends on the tolerance factor ϵ.)

To see this, consider an ϵ-bad rule: despite the efforts of an adversary, such a rule will disagree with examples with probability at least $\epsilon(1 - \eta)$. On the other hand, a correct hypothesis can be forced to disagree with examples with probability at most η. Provided $\eta < \epsilon(1 - \eta)$, we can modify Algorithm 5.1 to pac-identify the class, changing only the function m and the bounds on η and ϵ. Rearrange this inequality to obtain the stated condition.

Valiant [72] gives a polynomial-time algorithm, along the lines of Algorithm 5.16 above, for identifying $CNF_n k$ when the examples are subject to an ANP. His results hold for a rate of noise $\eta \leq \epsilon/4M$, where M is the number of clauses.

As another illustration, let us show how to identify $\odot$-normal form expressions efficiently from positive examples subject to an ANP. (This generalizes the $CNF_n(k)$ result obtained by Valiant in [72]). Correct components can be made to disagree with examples with probability at most η. To distinguish these from harmful components, we need a statistical separation from this probability.

So let us declare to be *harmful* any component that in the absense of noise disagrees on average with a fraction $> \epsilon/M$ of the examples, where M is the number of components. In the presence of noise, this rate might be reduced to $\epsilon(1-\eta)/M$ but no lower. Thus, provided $\eta < \epsilon(1-\eta)/M$. Our approach is to eliminate all harmful components while including all correct ones. Clearly the error in the resulting formula will then be at most ϵ.

Provided $\eta < \epsilon(1-\eta)/M$ (or, equivalently, $\eta < [(M/\epsilon)+1]^{-1}$), there is a separation of at least $s_b = \epsilon/M - \eta_b(1 + \epsilon/M)$ between the rate at which a harmful component is falsified and this rate for a correct component. Also, harmful components are falsified on average by a proportion of at least $\epsilon(1 - \eta_b)/M$ of the examples. Therefore we use the following algorithm:

1. Obtain a sample of $m = (2/s_b{}^2)\ln(M/\delta)$ positive examples.

2. Output the set ($\odot$-conjoined) of all components falsified by no more than $(\eta_b + s_b/2)m$ examples.

To see that this works, consider first *errors of omission* (discarding a correct component). For this to occur, the proportion of examples falsifying a correct component must exceed its expected value (η) by at least $s_b/2$; but m has been chosen so that the likelihood of this is at most δ/M.

Similarly, *errors of commission* (including a harmful component) occur only when a harmful component is falsified less often than expected, by a deviation of at least $s_b/2$. The chances of this are less than δ/M. Summing the probabilities of both types of errors over at most M components gives a probability for error of at most δ. Thus we have shown:

Theorem 5.29 Assume that the domain has an $\odot$-normal form property with M components that can be tested against examples in time polynomial in their size. Then there is an algorithm that runs in time polynomial in $1/\epsilon$, $\log 1/\delta$, $1/(1 - 2\eta_b)$, M, and the size of the examples and pac-identifies $\odot$-normal form formulas from positive examples subject to an ANP, provided the rate η of noise satisfies

$$\eta \leq \eta_b < \frac{1}{(M/\epsilon) + 1}.$$

Note that the family $CNF_n(k)$ satisfies the conditions of the theorem and hence is a polynomial-time identifiable family.

Bernoulli Noise. Both the CNP and ANP models require bounded noise rates in order for pac-identification to be possible in general. Is there a process for which an extremely high rate of noise can be tolerated without precluding identifiability? There is indeed. And in the noise process we now analyze, we are able to quantify the need for coding to limit the effects of noise.

Let us differentiate between two effects of noise on the examples. Suppose that as a result of noise an example $\langle s, x \rangle$ is changed to $\langle s', x' \rangle$, where s is the sign and x the content. If, as a result of noise, the sign of an example is reversed, we say that a *classification error* occurs in the example. If, apart from the sign, the body of the example is affected, we say that a *content error* occurs in the example as a result of noise. In general, both classification and content errors will affect an example. The *Bernoulli Noise Process* is one for which these errors are independently quantifiable.

Recently Valiant's results were extended by Kearns and Li [37]. They demonstrate upper limits on the tolerable error rate for many classes of logical formulas when positive and negative examples can be requested from separate sources, and each source of examples is independently subject to errors of the adversarial type. Their main result is that most classes of hypotheses are not learnable when the error rate is ϵ or higher. When only a single source (positive examples or negative, but not both) is available, the tolerable error rate is much lower – as low as $O(\epsilon/(N-1))$ for some classes with N formulas.

Definition 5.30 The *Bernoulli Noise Process* (BNP) is characterized by two parameters η_1 and η_2: Independently for each example, a classification error occurs with probability η_1; and independent of any classification error, a content error occurs with probability η_2.

This model may seem somewhat more contrived than the two previous ones, since we cannot easily envision a physical process that would independently affect the two parts of an example. The motivation behind the definition is that error-correcting codes can be used to limit the rate of occurrence of uncorrected faulty examples. If the sign and content portions of the example are encoded with differing amounts of redundancy, the effects of these two types of noise can be influenced independently, and the probabilities of classification and content errors may be different. As a result we can study the impact of content errors independently of classification errors.

Content errors can be particularly damaging to the identification process. Imagine two rules that differ only on a few high-probability examples; one of them, e_1, is a correct rule, and the other, e_2, is ϵ-bad. Substituting a positive example of both e_1 and e_2 for a positive example that supports e_1 but not e_2 can lend an unacceptable bias to the bad rule e_2, so that even a very small rate of content errors can be damaging if the particular errors are unfortunately chosen. Conversely, even a high rate of content noise in the examples can be supported if most of the errors merely substitute another example of the same rule, rather than an example of a different rule. Evidently, then, *the noise rate alone is not enough to determine the learnability of the class in the presence of content noise: we also need to quantify its severity.*

Let $P(e_1 \rightarrow e_2)$ be the conditional probability, given that a content error occurs in an example, that the content x of the example $\langle s, x \rangle$ belongs to e_1 before the error and the content x' belongs to e_2 after the error. Note that x' may also belong to e_1, but in general may not. In particular, if e and $\bar{e}$ are complementary rules, $P(e \rightarrow \bar{e})$ is the conditional probability that a content error changes an example of e to one no longer of e. The result is a counterexample of e if and only if the sign is reversed by the noise.

Recall that $P[S]$ is the probability of drawing an example x belonging to the set S before any noise occurs. U is the set of all possible examples; the rules denote subsets of U.

Definition 5.31 A noise process is said to satisfy the *bounded-content condition* if there exists a number λ, with $0 \leq \lambda < 1$, such that for any set $S \subseteq U$ of examples,

$$P(S \rightarrow \overline{S}) < \lambda P[S]. \tag{5.6}$$

Intuitively, if we focus on a particular set S and consider the proportion of examples that are in S before content errors and not in S after, then on average this fraction is bounded by λ, for *any* set S. How can we tell whether this condition holds? In practice, coding techniques would be used to ensure that it does. For example, suppose U is a finite set $\{x_1, \ldots, x_n\}$, and examples are encoded by a bit string representing the sign followed by a bit string representing an element $x \in U$. Assume that noise may complement each bit independently with probability p. For the empty set $S = \emptyset$, there are no examples in S, so the bounded-content condition (Eq. (5.6)) holds vacuously. When S is a singleton $\{x_i\}$, any undetected content error for the example x_i will displace the example from S to $\overline{S}$. The probability for this event depends on p and the encoding, and can be made smaller than any positive λ by increasing the redundancy in the code. When $|S| > 1$, the probability that a content error will displace the example from S to $\overline{S}$ is certainly no greater, so it follows that we can achieve the bounded-content condition with a suitable code.

The following theorem specifies the relative importance of the parameters λ, η_1, and η_2 in identification from examples littered with Bernoulli noise. Like previous conditions on the amount of noise, it takes the form of an inequality that, if satisfied, allows us to use our algorithm of sampling and choosing a least inconsistent rule.

Theorem 5.32 Let η_1 and η_2 be the parameters of a BNP with content error bounded by λ. Then *pac*-identification is possible provided

$$(1 - 2\eta_1)[\epsilon - \eta_2\lambda(\epsilon + 1)] > 0.$$

Before giving the proof, we note the following consequences:

1. If no content errors occur ($\eta_2 = 0$), this reduces to the condition that the classification noise rate be less than one half.

2. If no classification errors occur ($\eta_1 = 0$), identification is possible provided

$$\epsilon > \frac{\eta_2 \lambda}{1 - \eta_2 \lambda}.$$

Thus, even if $\eta_2 = 1$ (so that *every* example is affected by noise), identification is possible provided ϵ is not too small (and λ not too big).

PROOF: We calculate the probability that a good hypothesis e_t is contradicted by an example, and similarly for an ϵ-bad hypothesis e_i; then we determine when these probabilities are statistically separable.

For e_t the probability p_t of disagreement has three terms, depending on which types of noise occur:

$$
\begin{aligned}
p_t = \quad & \eta_1(1 - \eta_2) + & \text{(classification error only)} \\
& (1 - \eta_1)\eta_2[P(e_t \to \overline{e_t}) + P(\overline{e_t} \to e_t)] + & \text{(content error only)} \\
& \eta_1\eta_2[P(e_t \to e_t) + P(\overline{e_t} \to \overline{e_t})]. & \text{(both)}
\end{aligned}
$$

For example, consider the second term. If the example $\langle s, x \rangle$ suffers only from content errors, e_t will disagree with the resulting example $\langle s, x' \rangle$ either when x is in e_t and x' is in $\overline{e_t}$ (so that $s = +$), or when x is in $\overline{e_t}$ and x' is in e_t (so that $s = -$).

For any other hypothesis e_i, the probability p_i of disagreement has four terms:

$$
\begin{aligned}
p_i = \quad & (1 - \eta_1)(1 - \eta_2)P[e_i \triangle e_t] + & \text{(no error)} \\
& \eta_1(1 - \eta_2)[1 - P[e_i \triangle e_t]] + & \text{(classification error only)} \\
& (1 - \eta_1)\eta_2[P(e_t \to \overline{e_i}) + P(\overline{e_t} \to e_i)] + & \text{(content error only)} \\
& \eta_1\eta_2[P(e_t \to e_i) + P(\overline{e_t} \to \overline{e_i})]. & \text{(both)}
\end{aligned}
$$

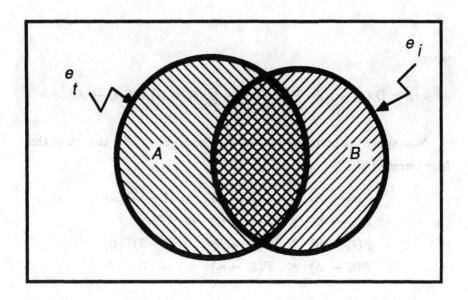

Figure 5.2: Illustrating sets A and B.

We now determine when $p_i - p_t > 0$ (the condition which enables us to differentiates e_i from e_t). By assumption, $P[e_i \triangle e_t] > \epsilon$. For convenience, let us introduce the sets $A = e_t - e_i$, $B = e_i - e_t$, and $C = \overline{e_t} \cap \overline{e_i}$. In terms of these sets, the expression $P(e_t \to \overline{e_i}) - P(e_t \to \overline{e_t})$ occurring in $p_i - p_t$ can be simplified as follows:

$$
\begin{aligned}
P(e_t \to \overline{e_i}) - P(e_t \to \overline{e_t}) &= (P(e_t \to A) + P(e_t \to C)) - \\
&\quad (P(e_t \to B) + P(e_t \to C)) \\
&= P(e_t \to A) - P(e_t \to B).
\end{aligned}
$$

Similarly, we can simplify

$$
P(\overline{e_t} \to e_i) - P(\overline{e_t} \to e_t) = P(\overline{e_t} \to B) - P(\overline{e_t} \to A).
$$

Thus (after some algebra) we obtain

$$
p_i - p_t > \epsilon(1 - \eta_2)(1 - 2\eta_1) + R\eta_2(1 - 2\eta_1),
$$

where

$$R = [P(e_t \to A) - P(e_t \to B)] + [P(\overline{e_t} \to B) - P(\overline{e_t} \to A)].$$

Now apply the bounded-content condition (Eq. (5.6)) to each of the four terms of R:

$$\begin{aligned}
P(e_t \to A) &\geq P(A \to A) &> (1 - \lambda)P[A] \\
P(e_t \to B) &\leq P(e_t \to \overline{e_t}) &< \lambda P[e_t] \\
P(\overline{e_t} \to B) &\geq P(B \to B) &> (1 - \lambda)P[B] \\
P(\overline{e_t} \to A) &\leq P(\overline{e_t} \to e_t) &< \lambda P[\overline{e_t}]
\end{aligned}$$

Substituting these inequalities into R, we obtain

$$\begin{aligned}
R &> (1 - \lambda)[P[A] + P[B]] - \lambda[P[e_t] + P[\overline{e_t}]] \\
&\geq (1 - \lambda)\epsilon - \lambda.
\end{aligned}$$

Finally,

$$p_i - p_t > (1 - 2\eta_1)[\epsilon - \eta_2\lambda(\epsilon + 1)].$$

When the righthand side is > 0, we have the condition stated in the theorem.

$\square$

5.8   Appendix to Chapter 5

We derive tighter bounds on the number of examples needed to pac-identify a finite set of rules (Section 5.4.1) with classification noise. The main results are as follows:

Theorem 5.33 Let $\eta < 1/2$ be the rate of classification noise and N the number of rules in the class $\mathcal{E}$. Assume $0 < \epsilon, \delta < \frac{1}{2}$. Then the number m of examples required is at least

$$m \geq \max \left[\frac{\ln(1/2\delta)}{\ln[1 - \epsilon(1 - 2\eta)]^{-1}}, \log_2 N (1 - 2\epsilon(1 - \delta) + 2\delta) \right] \quad (5.7)$$

and at most

$$m \leq \frac{\ln(N/\delta)}{\epsilon[1 - \exp[-\frac{1}{2}(1 - 2\eta)^2]]}. \quad (5.8)$$

More meaningful asymptotic forms of these functions for $\eta \to 0$ and $\eta \to 1/2$ are given below. The second expression in the *max* function in Eq. 5.7 is from [15] and is independent of noise.

In proof, we shall first derive as a lemma an exact expression for the number of examples. Then we use analytical techniques to bound this expression above and below.

As a lower bound, the number m must certainly be sufficient for the case when there are only two rules: one correct and one with error ϵ. We want to choose the correct rule by testing which one has the greater probability of agreeing with a random example. One can view this as a hypothesis-testing problem for which each round (i.e., drawing an example) has one of three possible outcomes:

1. The example agrees with the correct rule but not with the incorrect rule. The probability of this is $\epsilon(1 - \eta)$, since $(1 - \eta)$ is the probability that noise does not affect the example, and ϵ is the probability that the example contradicts the bad rule but not the good one. Such outcomes favor the good rule.

2. The example disagrees with the good rule but agrees with the bad one. The probability of this is $\epsilon\eta$. Such outcomes favor the bad

rule.

3. The example agrees with or disagrees with both rules, thereby offering no information about which is correct. The probability of this is $1 - \epsilon$.

Let K be the number of examples, out of m, for which either the first or second outcome occurs $(0 \leq K \leq m)$. If the second outcome occurs at least as often as the first, we may err by choosing the bad rule. So we must make the sample m large enough that this likelihood is less than δ. Given that one of the first two events occurs, the conditional probability of the first outcome is $1 - \eta$, and η for the second. Thus the conditional probability $\mathrm{Pr}_K(\text{wrong})$ that the first outcome occurs at most as often as the second is

$$\mathrm{Pr}_K(\text{wrong}) = \sum_{i=0}^{\lfloor K/2 \rfloor} \binom{K}{i}(1 - \eta)^i \eta^{K-i}$$
$$= LE(1 - \eta, K, \lfloor K/2 \rfloor / K).$$

Summing over the possible K, we obtain the total probability P that the bad rule will succeed at least as often as the good one:

$$P = \sum_{K=0}^{m} \binom{m}{K} \epsilon^K (1 - \epsilon)^{m-K} LE(1 - \eta, K, \lfloor K/2 \rfloor / K)$$
$$= \mathsf{E} \, LE(1 - \eta, K, \lfloor K/2 \rfloor / K),$$

where E indicates the mathematical expectation over the distribution of K, a sum of m Bernoulli random variables each with probability ϵ. It is this latter quantity that we shall bound.

Lower Bound. Since $\eta < \frac{1}{2}$,

$$LE(1 - \eta, K, \lfloor K/2 \rfloor /K) = \eta^K \sum_{i=0}^{\lfloor K/2 \rfloor} \binom{K}{i} \left(\frac{(1 - \eta)}{\eta} \right)^i$$

$$\geq \eta^K \sum_{i=0}^{\lfloor K/2 \rfloor} \binom{K}{i}$$

$$\geq \eta^K 2^{K-1}$$

$$= \frac{1}{2}(2\eta)^K$$

$$= \frac{1}{2} e^{K \ln(2\eta)}.$$

To compute the expectation of this, we note that the expected value of the moment-generating function of the random variable K satisfies

$$\mathsf{E}\, e^{sK} = [1 - \epsilon(1 - e^s)]^m.$$

Thus

$$\mathsf{E}\, LE(1 - \eta, K, \lfloor K/2 \rfloor /K) \geq \frac{1}{2} \mathsf{E}\, [1 - \epsilon(1 - e^{\ln(2\eta)})]^m$$

$$= \frac{1}{2}[1 - \epsilon(1 - 2\eta)]^m,$$

which we want to be less than δ. Such is the case when

$$m > \frac{\ln(1/2\delta)}{\ln[1 - \epsilon(1 - 2\eta)]^{-1}}.$$

Upper Bound. Note that $\lfloor K/2 \rfloor /K \leq 1/2$, so that $1 - \eta - (\lfloor K/2 \rfloor /K) \geq (1 - 2\eta)/2$. Applying Hoeffding's Inequality (Lemma 5.2) we find that

$$LE(1 - \eta, K, \lfloor K/2 \rfloor /K) \leq \exp\left[-K(1 - 2\eta)^2/2 \right].$$

As above, we can use the moment-generating function to compute the expectation of this quantity:

$$E\, LE(1 - \eta, K, \lfloor K/2 \rfloor / K) \;\leq\; [1 - \epsilon\alpha]^m$$
$$\leq\; e^{-\epsilon\alpha m},$$

where

$$\alpha \equiv 1 - \exp[-\frac{1}{2}(1 - 2\eta)^2].$$

This expression bounds the probability that a single ϵ-bad rule fails no more than a single good one. But we are seeking an upper bound, and with N rules, in the worst case there may be only one correct rule and $N - 1$ bad ones.

Taking

$$m = \frac{\ln(N/\delta)}{\epsilon\alpha},$$

we find that $e^{-\epsilon\alpha m} = \delta/N$; hence the probability of choosing a bad rule instead of a good one is $< \delta$. $\qquad\qquad\square$

Asymptotic values. More interesting than the formulas 5.7 and 5.8 are formulas showing the asymptotic dependency of m on the parameters ϵ, δ, and $1 - 2\eta$. We consider two cases:

- Very low noise ($\eta \to 0$). Since $\epsilon < \frac{1}{2}$, $\ln(1 - \epsilon)^{-1} \leq 2\epsilon \ln 2$. Thus from Eqn. 5.7 we have

$$m \geq \frac{1}{2\epsilon \ln 2} \ln\left(\frac{1}{2\delta}\right). \tag{5.9}$$

Also, $1/\alpha \to (1 - e^{-1/2})^{-1} < 8/3$, so from Eqn. 5.8 we have

$$m \leq \frac{8}{3\epsilon} \ln\left(\frac{N}{\delta}\right). \tag{5.10}$$

- Very high noise ($\eta \to \frac{1}{2}^-$). For the lower bound, we can bound $\ln[1 - \epsilon(1 - 2\eta)]^{-1}$ above by $2\epsilon(1 - 2\eta)\ln 2$: the latter is the linear function agreeing with the former at $\epsilon = 0$ and $\epsilon = 1/(2(1 - 2\eta)))$. With this we obtain from Eq. 5.7

$$m \geq \frac{1}{2\epsilon(1 - 2\eta)\ln 2} \ln\left(\frac{1}{2\delta}\right). \qquad (5.11)$$

To study Eq. 5.8 for noise rates near $1/2$, we expand α in a Taylor series about $(1 - 2\eta) = 0$ and obtain

$$\alpha \geq \frac{(1 - 2\eta)^2}{2} - \frac{(1 - 2\eta)^4}{8} + \mathcal{O}\left((1 - 2\eta)^6\right).$$

The following asymptotic upper bound follows:

$$m \sim \frac{2}{\epsilon(1 - 2\eta)^2} \ln\left(\frac{N}{\delta}\right). \qquad (5.12)$$

From these calculations we observe that m is $\Theta(\epsilon^{-1}\log(N/\delta)$, and with noise rates nearing $1/2$, m is $\Omega((1 - 2\eta)^{-1})$ and $\mathcal{O}((1 - 2\eta)^{-2})$.

It is instructive to examine some specific values from these formulas. Suppose the tolerance is $\epsilon = 0.1$, and the confidence rate $1 - \delta$ is to be 95%. With $N = 100$ rules, the maximum sample size needed for a noise rate approaching 0 is 194. With a noise rate of 1%, this number increases to 200.

Very high noise ($\gamma \approx \frac{1}{2}$). For the lower bound we can bound

and the following as an upper bound follows.

$$\left(\frac{|a|}{\sqrt{1-2\alpha}}\right)$$

Chapter 6

Conclusions

Let us summarize briefly the results presented in this dissertation, with an emphasis on how they related to one another. The model of the identification problem introduced in Chapter One has been used throughout, with variations in the nature of the presentation and criteria for convergence.

Chapters Two and Three have shown that there is nothing magical or mysterious about generalization or specialization operations and their use in identification algorithms. These relations have a simple algebraic structure. When some basic properties of the domain are known, we can readily construct refinement operators and prove their completeness. This ability represents an important advance over heuristic techniqes often described in the experimental literature.

The unifying notion of Chapters Four and Five is that of probability. Probability enters in two ways: in selecting examples at random, rather than by way of some arbitrary deterministic presentation; and in

197

allowing the algorithm to infer a rule with error that is probably very small. The selection of random examples reduces or eliminates the burden of having to remember every example seen so far, since possible examples will eventually recur with probability one. Allowing a bound on the error makes possible finite identification, even on infinite domains, and suggests useful measures of the complexity of identification. It also makes possible learning from noisy data.

A number of open problems have been mentioned in the text. Let us collect here the most interesting ones.

- Obtain efficient refinement algorithms. In pursuit of this, useful syntactic forms other than monotonic normal form might be found. Also, the extensive theory of term-rewriting systems might be applicable. An algorithm for *pac*-identification that utilizes refinement techniques would also be quite interesting.

- Find inductive biases automatically. The close relationship between inductive bias and universal refinements suggests further exploration of this idea.

- Devise other general strategies for identification from noisy data besides the "use the most consistent hypothesis" strategy.

- Determine the class of noise processes for which it is possible to estimate the rate of noise from the data.

- Find a class of rules and a type of noise for which polynomial-time identification is possible when the noise rate is below some threshold η; but when the noise is greater than η, the class is *pac*-identifiable but not in polynomial time. Alternately, prove that no such class exists: i.e., that any class learnable efficiently in the absense of noise is also learnable efficiently with noise, provided the rate of noise does not exceed the information-theoretic limit for learnability.

- Eliminate the requirement for models of pac-identification that the examples be independently random. Independence is a very difficult condition to ensure in practice.

Having worked so hard to arrive at this point, I feel I have earned the right to make some observations that are more editorial in content than scientific.

The nature of inductive inference by refinement (generalization and specialization) is now much more clearly understood, given the results of Chapters 2 and 3. But these results are disappointing in the sense that, as a general-purpose approach to inductive inference, traditional refinement methods are probably unsuitable. Either the algorithms are basically enumerative searches, or else special properties of the particular domain must be used in order to devise efficient refinement operators.

By contrast, probabilistic procedures can be efficient, with respect to both time (e.g., Example 4.6) and space (e.g., Algorithm 4.2). But the most recent results in this area suggest strongly that the choice of an appropriate representation is an essential element of this efficiency.

The results of Chapter 5 show that there is a general approach to handling noisy training examples. In the future it should become much more difficult to devise excuses for publishing noise-intolerant algorithms.

The major outstanding problem of "similarity-based" or "empirical" learning is that of learning a good bias and a good representation. Single instances of identification problems are not what intelligent beings are designed to solve; instead we perform much better over a range of problems to which our learning skills have become adapted. Evidently our brains are structured to extract regular patterns from mostly random sensory input and to formulate our search strategies with this knowledge as a basis. Interestingly, recent ethological studies with animals strongly suggest that many primitive forms of learning have built-in biases, in the sense that the animals are "hard-wired" to learn particular rules and not others ([25]). We should view these biases as having been "learned" by evolution over periods of time measured in generations.

Finally, progress in the fundamental understanding of learning will benefit from a symbiosis between mathematical and experimental research. Unfortunately, the theoreticians have tended to disregard the work of experimentalists, usually on esthetic grounds. Experimentalists commonly dismiss the theory as irrelevant and criticize theorists for solving the wrong problems. Those of us who traverse the boundaries typically pay a price for the effort.

Recently, however, there are signs that cooperative research between groups with different perspectives can be very productive. I expect that the growing interest in and importance of the subject of learning will greatly encourage this trend.

Bibliography

[1] Aho, A. V., J. E. Hopcroft, and J. D. Ullman. *The design and analysis of computer algorithms.* Reading, Mass.: Addison–Wesley, 1974.

[2] Angluin, D. Finding patterns common to a set of strings. *J.CSS:21* 46-62, 1980.

[3] Angluin, D. Learning regular sets from queries and counterexamples. Yale Univ. Tech. Report. 464, 1986 (submitted).

[4] Angluin, D. Queries and concept learning. To appear in *Machine Learning.*

[5] Angluin, D. Learning k-bounded context-free grammars. Yale University Technical Report 557. August, 1987.

[6] Angluin, D. and P. D. Laird. Identifying k-CNF formulas from noisy examples. Yale Univ. Tech. Report. 478, 1986.

[7] Angluin, D. and P. D. Laird. Learning from noisy examples. Manuscript, submitted.

[8] Angluin, D. and C. H. Smith. Inductive Inference: theory and methods. *Computing Surveys 15*:237-269, September, 1983.

201

[9] Banerji, R. The logic of learning. In *Advances in Computers* *24*:177-216, 1985.

[10] Banerji, R. Learning in a growing language. preprint, 1987. To appear.

[11] Birkhoff, G. and S. MacLane. *A survey of modern algebra.* 4th Edition, New York: Macmillan, 1977.

[12] Biermann, A. and J. Feldman. On the synthesis of finite-state machines from samples of their behavior. *IEEE Trans. Comput.* *C-21*:592-597, 1972.

[13] Blum, M. A machine-independent theory of the complexity of recursive functions. *JACM 14*:2 (322–336), 1967.

[14] Blum, L. and M. Blum. Toward a mathematical theory of inductive inference. *Information and Control 28*: 125–155, 1975.

[15] Blumer, A., A. Ehrenfeucht, D. Haussler, and M. Warmuth. Classifying geometric concepts with the Vapnik-Chervonenkis dimension. *Proc. 18th Sym. Th. Comp.*:273-282, 1986. Submitted.

[16] Blumer, A., A. Ehrenfeucht, D. Haussler, and M. Warmuth. Occam's Razor. *Inf. Proc. Let.*, to appear, 1986.

[17] Bruner, J., J. Goodnow, and G. Austin. *A Study of Thinking* New York: Wiley, 1956.

[18] Buntine, W. Generalised subsumption and its applications to induction and redundancy. Tech. Rep. TR 86.3, New South Wales Inst. of Tech., 1986.

[19] Case, J. and C. H. Smith. Comparison of identification criteria for Machine Inductive Inference. *Theoretical Computer Science 25*: 193-220, 1983.

[20] Cohn, P. *Universal Algebra.* Dordrecht: D. Reidel, 1981.

[21] Daley, R. and C. Smith. On the complexity of inductive inference. Tech. Rpt. 83-4, Department of Computer Science, University of Pittsburgh. 1983.

[22] Dietterich, T. and R. Michalski. A comparative review of selected methods for learning from examples. In *Machine Learning, An Artificial Intelligence Approach*. Los Altos, California: Morgan Kaufmann, 1983.

[23] Feller, W. *An Introduction to Probability Theory and its Applications*, 3rd Edition. New York: J. Wiley and Sons, 1968.

[24] Gold, E. M. Language identification in the limit. *Information and Control 10*: 447–474, 1967.

[25] Gould, J. L. and P. Marler. Learning by Instinct. *Scientific American 256*: 74-85, January, 1987.

[26] Haussler, D. Storage efficient learning algorithms. Unpublished manuscript - 1985.

[27] Haussler, D. Quantifying the inductive bias in concept learning. Tech. Rep. UCSC-CRL-86-25. University of California, Santa Cruz, 1986.

[28] Haussler, D. Bias and Valiant's Learning Framework. *Proc. 4th Mach. Learning Workshop*: 324-336, 1987.

[29] Hayes-Roth, F. and J. McDermott. Knowledge acquisition from structural descriptions. *IJCAI Proceedings 5*:356-362, 1977.

[30] W. Hoeffding. Probability inequalities for sums of bounded random variables. *J. Amer. Stat. Assoc.*, 58:13–30, 1963.

[31] Hopcroft, J. E. and J. D. Ullman. *Introduction to automata theory, languages, and computation*. Reading, Mass.: Addison–Wesley, 1979

[32] Horning, J. J. A study of grammatical inference. Ph.D. dissertation, Computer Science Dept., Stanford University. 1969.

[33] Hunt, E., J. Marin, and P. Stone. *Experiments in Induction* New York: Academic Press, 1966.

[34] Huntbach, M. Program synthesis by inductive inference. pre-print, University of Sussex, Brighton BN1 9QN, U.K., 1987.

[35] Ishizaka, H. Model Inference Incorporating Generalization. *Proc. Symp. on Software Science and Engineering*, Kyoto, Sept., 1986.

[36] Kearns, M., M. Li, L. Pitt, and L. Valiant. On the learnability of Boolean formulae. *Proc. 19th STOC*, June, 1987.

[37] Kearns, M. and M. Li. Learning in the presence of malicious errors. Tech. Rep. TR-03-87, Harvard University, 1987.

[38] Knobe, B. and K. Knobe. A method for inferring context-free grammars. *Information and Control 31*:129-146, 1976.

[39] Laird, P. Inductive Inference by Refinement. Tech. Rep. 376, Yale University, 1986.

[40] Laird, P. Inductive Inference by Refinement. *AAAI-86 Proceedings*: 472-476. 1986.

[41] Laird, P. and L. Pitt. Finding an optimal search strategy for a partial order is NP-Complete. Tech. Rep. 493, Yale University, 1986.

[42] Machtey, M. and P. Young. *An Introduction to the General Theory of Algorithms*. New York: Elsevier North-Holland, 1978.

[43] Marron, A. and K. Ko. Identification of pattern languages from examples and queries. University of Houston, Tech. Rep. UH-CS-85-6, 1985.

[44] Minicozzi, E. Some natural properties of strong identification in inductive inference. *Theoretical Computer Science 2*:345-360, 1976.

[45] Michalski, R. A theory and methodology of inductive learning. In *Machine Learning*, Los Altos: Morgan Kaufmann, 1983.

[46] Mitchell, T. M. Version Spaces: an approach to concept learning. Ph.D. dissertation, Stanford University, 1978.

[47] Mitchell, T. M. The need for biases in learning generalizations. Rutgers University, Tech. Rep. CBM-TR-117, 1980.

[48] Mitchell, T. M. Generalization as search. *Artificial Intelligence 18*: 203–226,1982.

[49] Pao,T. W. and J. W. Carr, III. A solution of the syntactical induction-inference problem for regular languages. *Comput. Lang. 3*: 53-64, 1978.

[50] Pitt, L. and L. Valiant. Computational limitations on learning from examples. Harvard Univ., Tech. Rep. TR-05-86, 1986.

[51] Plotkin, G. D. A note on inductive generalization. In *Machine Intelligence 5*: 153-163. New York: Elsevier North-Holland, 1970.

[52] Plotkin, G. D. A further note on inductive generalization. In *Machine Intelligence 6*: 101-124. Edinburgh Univ. Press, 1971.

[53] Quinlan, J. R. Learning efficient classification procedures and their application to chess end games. In *Machine Learning*, Morgan Kaufmann, Los Altos, 1983.

[54] Quinlan, J. R. The effect of noise on concept learning. In *Machine Learning II*, Los Altos: Morgan Kaufmann, 1986.

[55] Red'ko, V. N. Relational definitions for the algebra of regular events. *Ukrain. Math. Zh. 16*: 120–126, 1964. (In Russian)

[56] Rendell, L., R. Seshu, and D. Tcheng. More robust concept learning using dynamically-variable bias. *Proc. 4th Int. Workshop on Machine Learning*, Morgan Kaufmann, 1987.

[57] Reynolds, J. C. Transformational systems and the algebraic structure of atomic formula. In *Machine Intelligence 5*, B. Meltzer and D. Mitchie, Eds. Edinburgh University Press, Edinburgh, 1970.

[58] Robinson, J. A. A machine-oriented logic based on the resolution principle. *J. ACM 12*: 23–41, 1965.

[59] Rudich, S. Inferring the structure of a Markov chain from its output. *Proc. 26th FOCS*: 321–325, 1985.

[60] Salomaa, A. Two complete axiom systems for the algebra of regular events. *J.ACM 13*: 158–169, 1966.

[61] Schäfer, G. Some results in the theory of effective program synthesis: learning by defective information. In *Mathematical Methods of Specification and Synthesis of Software Systems '85, Proceedings*, W. Bibel and K. Jantke, eds. *Lecture Notes in Computer Science: 215*, Berlin: Springer-Verlag, 1986.

[62] Schäfer, G. Über Eingabeabhängigkeit und Komplexität von Inferenzstrategien. Ph.D. Dissertation, RWTH Aachen, 1984.

[63] Schlimmer, J. and D. Fisher. A case study of incremental concept induction. *Proc. AAAI-86*:496–501, 1986.

[64] Schlimmer, J. and R. Granger. Beyond incremental processing: tracking concept drift. *Proc. AAAI-86*:502–507, 1986.

[65] Shapiro, E. Y. Inductive inference of theories from facts. Tech. Rep. 192, Department of Computer Science, Yale University, New Haven, Ct. 1981

[66] Shapiro, E. Y. Algorithmic program debugging. Ph. D. dissertation, Computer Science Department, Yale University, New Haven, Ct. 1982. Published by M.I.T. Press, 1983.

[67] Shinohara, T. Study on Inductive Inference from Positive Data. Ph.D. Dissertation, Kyushu Univ., 1986.

[68] Shiryayev, A. *Probability*. New York: Springer-Verlag, 1984.

[69] Utgoff, P. Shift of bias for inductive concept learning. Ph.D. dissertation, Rutgers Univ., 1984. Published by Kluwer Academic Press.

[70] Utgoff, P. Shift of bias for inductive concept learning. In *Machine Learning II*, Los Altos: Morgan Kaufmann, 1986.

[71] Valiant, L. G. A theory of the learnable. *C. ACM 27*: 1134–1142, November, 1984.

[72] L. G. Valiant. Learning disjunctions of conjunctions. In *Proceedings of IJCAI*: 560–566, IJCAI, 1985.

[73] Van der Mude, A. Some formal properties of version spaces. Tech. Rep. DCS-TR-201, Rutgers Univ., 1986.

[74] V. Vapnik. *Estimation of Dependencies Based on Empirical Data*. Springer-Verlag, 1982.

[75] Wilkins, D. and B. Buchanan. On debugging rule sets when reasoning under uncertainty. *Proc. AAAI-86*: 448-454, 1986.

[76] Yokomori, Takashi. Inductive inference of context-free languages – context-free expression method. Res. Rept. 71, International Institutue for Advanced Study of Social Information Science, Namazu, Japan, 1986.

Index